Pupus

An Island Tradition

Sachi Fukuda

3565 Harding Ave.
Honolulu, Hawai'i 96816
Phone: (800) 910-2377
Fax: (808) 732-3627
www.besspress.com

Cover design: Carol Colbath

Sachi Fukuda
        Pupus: An Island Tradition
Honolulu: Hawaii: Bess Press, Inc.
184 pages

Copyright © 1995 by Bess Press, Inc.
ALL RIGHTS RESERVED
Printed in the United States of America
ISBN: 1-57306-019-4

This book is dedicated to our first grandchild, Alysa Mika Wagatsuma, who has provided Lynn and me with an opportunity to watch and participate in her growth and development. She made us realize that we missed this with our children because we were focusing on our work and everyday living (and we had an excellent baby-sitter) while they were growing up.

We are grateful for this second chance. Thank you, Mika-chan!

INTRODUCTION

Pupus are an island tradition. They are so much a part of our island living that many gatherings are "heavy pupus"-type affairs.

Islanders transplanted on the mainland and elsewhere cling to island traditions, and preparing and serving pupus to their friends is a wonderful way of doing this.

Wherever you live, these recipes, collected, concocted, tested and adapted over a period of 20 years, offer a variety of flavorful pupus for your island-style entertaining.

DIPS AND SPREADS

BREADS AND CHEESE PASTRY

MUSHROOMS

CONTENTS

VEGETABLES

CONTENTS

MEATS

HEALTHY PUPUS

MISCELLANEOUS

DIPS & SPREADS

HOT BROCCOLI DIP

4 scallions, diced
2 Tbsp. butter
1 pkg. frozen broccoli, chopped
1 can cream of mushroom soup
1/4 lb. fresh mushrooms, chopped
8 oz. Cheddar cheese, grated
1/4 tsp. garlic salt
3 dashes Tabasco
1/4 tsp. pepper
1/2 cup toasted slivered almonds
1 loaf thin-sliced Pepperidge Farm bread

Thaw and drain broccoli.

Trim crusts from bread and cut into squares or triangles. Bake in 250° oven for 1 hour.

Sauté scallions in butter. Mix in remaining ingredients and cook on low heat, stirring frequently until mixture boils.

Transfer to chafing dish and serve hot. Use toasted bread squares for dipping.

NOTE: This can also be used as a dip for raw vegetables.

VEGETABLE CHEESE DIP

1 5-oz. jar Kraft Old English sharp cheese
1 cup mayonnaise, cold
Cucumbers, carrots, celery, cauliflower, mushrooms, etc.

Melt cheese in small saucepan over very low heat and when completely melted, immediately mix into the mayonnaise and refrigerate. Serve with julienne strips of assorted vegetables.

Note: This recipe originally called for other seasoning, but I found it unnecessary. This is so good and fast and delicious. A good way to get your children to eat vegetables. An old University Extension recipe that has been resurrected and is enjoying new popularity.

8-LAYER DIP

1 can jalapeño bean dip
1 large avocado, mashed with 1 tsp. lemon juice
    and green taco sauce to taste
3 Tbsp. mayonnaise
3 Tbsp. sour cream
1 Tbsp. chili powder
1 cup Jack cheese, grated
1 cup Cheddar cheese, grated
2–3 cups chopped firm tomatoes
4 stalks green onion, chopped
1 small can chopped olives

Spread jalapeño bean dip on large flat serving dish. Cover with seasoned mashed avocado.

Cover this with mixture of mayonnaise, sour cream and chili powder. Add Jack and Cheddar cheeses.

Cover with chopped tomatoes and green onion. Top with chopped olives. Use taco or corn chips for dipping.

NOTE: Have a spoon handy to scoop this delicious dip onto the taco or corn chips. The dip is quite stiff and heavy, so the spoon will help.

VERY BEST HOT BEAN DIP

1 10-1/2-oz. can jalapeño bean dip
8 oz. sour cream
8 oz. cream cheese, softened
1/2 pkg. taco seasoning mix
1/8 tsp. Tabasco
3 oz. Monterey Jack cheese, grated
3 oz. Cheddar cheese, grated
1 ripe avocado, diced
1 medium tomato, diced and drained
1/4 cup green pepper, diced
1/2 cup black olives, sliced (optional)
Tortilla chips

Mix first 5 ingredients and spread in a baking dish. Top with grated cheeses.

Bake at 350° for 15-20 minutes until heated through. Remove from oven.

Top with avocado, tomatoes, green pepper and olives. Dip with regular tortilla chips.

NOTE: Serve with a spoon to be used for scooping this delicious dip onto the tortilla chips. It is not soft like most dips, so the chips tend to break. Most adults love this south-of-the-border dip.

GLORIOUS MUSHROOM SPREAD

2 Tbsp. butter
1 lb. fresh mushrooms, diced
1 large onion, chopped
1-1/2 cups mayonnaise
10 strips bacon, crisped, crumbled
1/2 tsp. seasoned salt
1/2 cup Cheddar cheese, grated (optional)

In large skillet, sauté mushrooms in butter 3-5 minutes. Combine with remaining ingredients and bake in flat ovenproof dish at 350° for 20-25 minutes. Spread on cocktail rye rounds or crackers. May be assembled up to 2 days ahead and heated before serving.

NOTE: Freezes well. Thaw, warm and serve.

CHEESE JELLY SPREAD

8 oz. cream cheese, softened
1 10-oz. jar pineapple preserve
1 10-oz. jar apple jelly
3-4 Tbsp. horseradish
White pepper to taste

Blend above ingredients except cream cheese and pour over softened block of cream cheese. Serve with wheat crackers.

NOTE: There should be enough horseradish so you can taste it. This is a refreshing, delicious dish that can even be used as a dessert.

It makes a large quantity, so you may want to halve the recipe if serving a small group.

HOT CLAM SPREAD

2 7-1/2-oz. cans minced clams with juice
1 cup bread crumbs
1/2 cup butter, melted
1/2 tsp. oregano
1/2 tsp. parsley flakes
Dash of garlic salt
Dash of salt and pepper
4 oz. Mozzarella cheese, grated
1/2 cup Parmesan cheese

Combine all ingredients, except cheese. Place in 9-inch ovenproof dish, sprinkle with cheese, and bake at 350° for 15 minutes. Serve with crackers.

HOT CRAB DIP

8 oz. cream cheese
2 Tbsp. mayonnaise
2 Tbsp. evaporated milk
8 oz. flaked crabmeat, fresh frozen
2 Tbsp. finely chopped onion
1/2 tsp. cream-style horseradish
1/4 tsp. salt
1/4 tsp. Worcestershire sauce
Dash of pepper

Mix softened cream cheese with mayonnaise and milk. Add remaining ingredients and bake at 375° for 20-25 minutes until edges are golden brown. Serve with crackers or chips.

Note: Chopped fresh shrimp added to the above is also very good. This is a favorite of our family and friends.

AVOCADO-CRAB DIP

1 large avocado, diced
1 Tbsp. fresh lemon juice
2 Tbsp. grated onion
1 Tbsp. Worcestershire sauce
4 oz. cream cheese, softened
1/2 cup sour cream
1/2 tsp. salt
1 7-1/2-oz. can crabmeat, drained and flaked

Mix diced avocado with lemon juice, onion and Worcestershire sauce. Stir in cream cheese, sour cream and salt. Add crabmeat and mix thoroughly.

Serve with tortilla chips or crackers.

NOTE: Use firm avocado to avoid a messy-looking dip and toss rather than mix with lemon juice, etc. Blend the cream cheese, sour cream and salt, add the crabmeat and fold carefully into the seasoned avocado.

You will enjoy this once you get past its looks. Good change of pace from the usual Guacamole Dip, which everyone prepares whenever avocados are plentiful.

CRAB SPREAD

1 pint mayonnaise
4 Tbsp. ketchup
1 Tbsp. Parmesan cheese
1 tsp. A-1 sauce
1/2 tsp. curry powder
1 lb. crabmeat, fresh frozen

Mix well and chill. Serve with crackers.

IMITATION CRAB DIP

1/2 lb. imitation crab
1/2 cup small-curd cottage cheese
1 cup mayonnaise
1/2 tsp. seasoned salt
1 2-oz. pkg. Ranch Style dressing mix
1/2 tsp. garlic salt

Cut artificial crab strips into 1-inch pieces. Shred. Mix with remaining ingredients, chill and serve with crackers or vegetable sticks.

CRAB DIP

24 oz. cream cheese, softened
1/2 cup mayonnaise
1/4 cup dry white wine
2 Tbsp. Dijon mustard
1-1/2 tsp. powdered sugar
1 tsp. grated onion

2 cloves garlic, pressed
1 lb. flaked crabmeat, fresh frozen
1/2 cup toasted, slivered almonds
1/4 cup minced fresh parsley

Thoroughly combine cheese, mayonnaise, wine, mustard, sugar, onion and garlic. Fold in crab and heat. Transfer to warm chafing dish and sprinkle with almonds and parsley. Serve with crackers. May also be served cold.

SHRIMP DIP

1/2 cup cooked shrimp, chopped fine
3 oz. cream cheese
1-1/2 tsp. anchovy paste
3 Tbsp. mayonnaise

Blend all ingredients together. Spread on toast or crackers or use as dip for chips.

Note: This is one of the first recipes I ever received. It is still one of my favorites.

COLD SHRIMP DIP

8-oz. cream cheese
1 cup small shrimp, cooked
1/4 cup mayonnaise
1/2 cup chili sauce
1/4 cup grated onion
3 drops Tabasco
1/2 tsp. Worcestershire sauce

Beat cream cheese until smooth, fold in remaining ingredients and mix until well blended. Refrigerate for several hours. Serve with Ritz crackers or raw vegetables.

NOTE: Freezes well. Handy for unexpected company.

SALMON PARTY LOG

1-lb. can salmon
1/4 tsp. salt
3 Tbsp. snipped parsley
2 tsp. grated onion
1 cup chopped pecans
8 oz. cream cheese, softened

1/4 tsp. liquid smoke
1 Tbsp. lemon juice
1 tsp. horseradish
1/2 tsp. garlic salt
1/2 tsp. seasoned salt
1 tsp. Pickapeppa

Drain salmon well. Bone and flake. Combine everything except parsley and nuts. Roll into log shape, using heavy waxed paper to help you roll. Chill several hours. If it does not harden, freeze until firm and then put back into refrigerator. Keeps well for several days. Roll hardened log in nuts and parsley that have been well mixed.

NOTE: Substituting macadamia nuts will give it a typical island flavor.

SALMON CHEESE MOLD

1/2 cup tomato soup
8 oz. cream cheese
1/2 cup mayonnaise
1 can salmon, drained
1 pkg. unflavored gelatin softened
    in 1/4 cup water

1 small onion, chopped
1/4 cup celery, chopped
1/4 cup green pepper,
chopped
1/4 tsp. salt
1/4 tsp. garlic salt

Heat soup. Dissolve cream cheese in soup and add gelatin to dissolve. Cool, add remaining ingredients and pour into mold and refrigerate. Serve with crackers.

NOTE: The original recipe called for canned shrimp. It was too bland, so I substituted salmon.

LOMI SALMON DIP

1/2 lb. salted salmon
1 small round onion
2 firm medium tomatoes
Poi

Rinse salmon a few times and soak at least 2 hours. Drain and remove skin and bones. Cut salmon into 1/4- to 1/2-inch strips and then into cubes.

Cut round onion and tomatoes into similar-sized cubes.

Use 6-inch skewers and skewer a piece of onion, a piece of tomato and then a piece of salmon.

Place in spoke fashion on a flat platter with a small bowl of mixed poi in the center for dipping.

NOTE: It is amazing how much like lomi salmon this dip will taste in spite of looking completely different. The only thing missing is the green onion. Poi is a very good dip. Who would have thought that it could be used like this?

BAGNA CAUDA

1/2 lb. butter
1/2 cup olive oil
4-8 cloves of garlic, puréed or minced
2 cans anchovy fillets, minced

Heat all of the above gently for 10 minutes in a fondue pot or slow cooker in which you will serve this sauce. Cut assorted raw vegetables such as carrots, cauliflower, broccoli, mushrooms, cucumbers, etc., to be dipped into this sauce.

NOTE: This is a delicious way to serve raw vegetables. Stir the bottom of the pot occasionally so the fillets won't sink to the bottom and cause the heating element to overheat and boil over. The remaining sauce is so delicious that my friend pours it over her rice.

LOBSTER SPREAD

2 cups lobster, finely chopped
1/2 cup mayonnaise
1 Tbsp. A-1 sauce
1 tsp. chopped green onion
1/2 tsp. lemon juice
Salt and paprika to taste

Mix all of the above ingredients and serve with Wheat Thins or other cocktail crackers or bread.

NOTE: This can be served hot by adding 1/4 cup mayonnaise and baking at 350° for 20-25 minutes. Good both hot or cold.

KAMABOKO DIP

2 kamaboko (fish cake)
1/3 cup mayonnaise
Round onion
1/4 tsp. garlic salt

Grate the kamaboko. Mix with mayonnaise and grate 1/3 to 1/4 of a medium round onion. Add garlic salt. Serve with crackers or chips.

NOTE: You will swear this was made with shrimp.

ANCHOVY VEGETABLE DIP

2 cans flat anchovy fillets, well drained
1/4 cup red wine vinegar
3/4 cup olive oil
4 cloves garlic, minced or pressed
1/4 tsp. pepper
1/2 cup parsley, chopped

Place anchovies and vinegar in blender and whirl until puréed. Add oil, garlic and pepper; whirl until smoothly blended; stir in parsley.

Transfer to a serving bowl; cover and chill at least 2 hours. Yields 2 cups.

NOTE: Good with celery and cucumber sticks, radishes, cherry tomatoes, whole mushrooms, broccoli and cauliflower. Chill vegetables also until serving time.

The original recipe called for 3 cans of anchovies, which was too salty for my taste, so I cut it down to 2 cans.

BREADS & CHEESE PASTRY

PARMESAN FRENCH BREAD

1 loaf French bread
1/2 block butter, melted
1/4 cup chopped round onion
1 cup mayonnaise
Dash Worcestershire Sauce

Split French bread almost completely through lengthwise. Coat two halves with melted butter. Slice each half loaf almost completely through so you can easily tear off the slices. Coat each slice with mixture of chopped onion, mayonnaise and Worcestershire sauce. Sprinkle 1 medium can of Parmesan cheese heavily over top of mayonnaise mixture. Place on cookie sheet and bake in 350° oven for 15 minutes or until light and bubbly.

CHEESE-PUFF PASTE

1/4 lb. butter
1/4 lb. cottage cheese
1-1/2 cups flour

Mix all ingredients well. Roll out thin and cut into 2-inch squares. Fill each with one teaspoon of your favorite meat filling, fold over and crimp edges by pressing together with fork to seal. Bake at 350° for 20 minutes.

NOTE: This is a very flaky pastry that can also be used as a dessert by simply filling it with jam or any type of sweet filling.

PINT-SIZED PIZZAS

1 8-oz. can tomato sauce
1/2 tsp. oregano
1/4 tsp. garlic salt
1/4 tsp. black pepper
6 oz. bologna, scored and sliced thin
1 cup grated Mozzarella cheese
1 loaf French bread, sliced

Combine first four ingredients; mix well. Spread sliced bread with mixture. Top bread with bologna; sprinkle with grated cheese. Broil 2 to 4 minutes or until cheese melts or bake at 425° for approximately 20 minutes.

PORTUGUESE MINI-PIZZA

8 hot dog buns
1/2 cup grated Cheddar cheese
1/2 cup round onion, chopped
2 green onion stalks, chopped
3/4 cup mayonnaise
2 Tbsp. chopped parsley
3/4 Portuguese sausage, boiled and chopped

Cut hot dog buns through to make 16 half buns. Mix remaining ingredients and spread on half bun. Broil for a few minutes, being careful not to burn the cheese. Cut each half bun into four pieces.

NOTE: You should be able to get 64 bite-sized pieces. This can be made and frozen until ready to use. Broil until the cheese melts, being careful not to burn it. The sausage is already cooked, so there is no danger of undercooking it.

MINI SHRIMP TARTLETS

Pastry:
1/2 cup butter
3 oz. cream cheese
1 cup flour

Beat together butter and cream cheese until smooth. Add flour and form into a ball. Wrap in waxed paper and chill for 30 minutes or longer. Pastry can be made a day ahead. Make miniature pie shells by shaping the dough into 1-inch balls and pressing it into the bottom and sides of small muffin cups about 1-1/2 inches in diameter.

Filling:
4 ounces small cooked shrimp
1 medium shrimp
1 medium onion, chopped and
  lightly sautéed
1/2 cup grated Swiss cheese

2 eggs, slightly beaten
1/2 cup milk
1/8 tsp. nutmeg
Black pepper

Preheat oven to 450°. In each miniature pie shell place a few small shrimp, then a little sautéed chopped bacon, anything. Artichoke nibbles can also be placed in the shell and baked. Add bread crumbs on top before baking.

Note: These can be frozen after baking and reheated at 450° for 10 minutes directly from the freezer. Filling can be made substituting crab, canned clams, chopped cooked ham, sautéed chopped bacon, anything. Artichoke nibbles can also be placed in the shell and baked. Add bread crumbs on top before baking.

MUSHROOM ROLL-UPS

1 can cream of mushroom soup
1 4-oz. can mushroom stems and pieces
1/2 loaf sliced white bread
4 Tbsp. melted butter

Drain liquid and chop mushroom stems and pieces. Add to undiluted cream of mushroom soup. Cut crust off four sides of bread and roll each slice flat with rolling pin. Place about 2 tablespoons of soup mixture on the edge nearest you and spread it over two-thirds of the bread. Roll from that edge to the opposite end as you would in making sushi. Place seam side down on cookie sheet and place in freezer for at least 2 hours or overnight.

Cut rolls into thirds, brush with melted butter and bake for 15-20 minutes in 375° oven until slightly toasty.

NOTE: Do not let rolls thaw while heating the oven. The original recipe called for fresh mushrooms cooked lovingly with a sauce, but the end result tasted like cream of mushroom soup. I have since used the soup and just added more mushrooms. Definitely easier and faster. This is another recipe that freezes nicely for weeks. You have pupus to serve at a moment's notice.

STUFFED FRENCH BREAD

1 small loaf French bread
8 oz. cream cheese
6 oz. crabmeat
3 Tbsp. chopped parsley
Mayonnaise to moisten

Cheese spread:
2 cups sharp Cheddar cheese, grated
2 Tbsp. softened butter

Blend cheese and butter until smooth.

Preheat oven to 350°. Cut French bread in half, lengthwise. Remove some of the bread in the center to make a shallow trench in each half. Cover each trench with cheese spread. Add mayonnaise to crabmeat to moisten and spread over the cheese. Bake for 20 minutes or until bubbly. Sprinkle with chopped parsley and cut into serving pieces.

CHEDDAR ROUNDS

6 oz. Cheddar cheese
1 block margarine
1 cup flour
1/2 tsp. salt
1 Tbsp. toasted sesame seeds
Paprika
Cayenne

Work cheese and margarine until creamy. Mix flour, salt, sesame seeds, dash of paprika and cayenne into cheese mixture by hand and work until smooth. Pinch off dough and roll into 3/4- to 1-inch balls. Place on ungreased cookie sheet and press each ball with greased glass or cup dipped in flour to flatten slightly. Bake at 350° for 15 minutes.

WHOLE WHEAT LAVOSH

3 cups whole wheat flour
1 block margarine
3/4 cup water
1/3 cup powdered milk
1/4 cup sugar
1/2 tsp. salt
1/2 tsp. baking soda
4 Tbsp. sesame seed

Heat margarine and water until melted. Add all other ingredients and mix well, finishing off by kneading dough for one minute. Pinch off walnut-sized balls and roll thin. Bake on ungreased cookie sheet at 375° for 10-12 minutes, turning once to brown evenly.

NOTE: Can also be baked in large sheets, cutting off excess that doesn't fit on cookie sheet and placing them on another sheet to bake. Large sheets can be broken into 3- x 5-inch pieces when cooled and stored in airtight containers. They keep well and are excellent with wine and cheese. They also make very good sandwiches when spread with tuna or egg salad. Very nutritious and very good as a plain snack.

HOT BOLOGNA ROUNDS

10 oz. bologna, coarsely ground
1 cup grated American cheese
2 Tbsp. chopped green pepper
3 Tbsp. chopped green onion
4 Tbsp. catsup
6 hamburger buns

Mix all ingredients except hamburger buns. Spread mixture on both halves of the hamburger buns. Broil several minutes until hot and bubbly. Cut into halves or quarters before serving.

MUSHROOMS

MUSHROOMS STUFFED WITH SHRIMP

2 Tbsp. butter, melted
12 large mushrooms, cleaned, with stems removed
12 medium shrimp, cooked, deveined and chopped
1 Tbsp. chives, finely chopped
1 clove garlic, finely diced
1 Tbsp. cooking Sherry
1/4 cup bread crumbs
1/4 tsp. salt
Parmesan cheese
Paprika

Dip mushroom caps in melted butter and set aside in greased pan.

Fry chopped mushroom stems, shrimp, chives and garlic in remaining butter until mushrooms are tender, about 3 minutes. Add sherry and stir. Add salt and enough bread crumbs to hold mixture together.

Stuff the mushroom caps with mixture. Sprinkle tops with Parmesan cheese and paprika. Broil until hot and nicely browned.

NOTE: Mushroom lovers and shrimp lovers will really go for this dish. Not only is it delicious, but it is also easy to prepare.

STUFFED BLACK MUSHROOMS

24 medium dried black mushrooms (shiitake)
1/2 lb. fresh shrimp
1/2 tsp. salt
1/2 white onion, minced
1/4 cup fresh coriander, minced
1 tsp. ginger, finely minced
1 egg, lightly beaten
1/2 lb. ground pork
1/2 tsp. salt
1 tsp. sesame oil
1/2 tsp. pepper
1 Tbsp. Sherry
1 Tbsp. oyster sauce

Soak dried mushrooms in warm water about 30 minutes. Squeeze out excess water; cut off stems. Shell and devein shrimp. Put shrimp in bowl with 1/2 teaspoon salt and gently mix with fingers. Rinse several times and drain well. Mince shrimp, onion, coriander and ginger. Beat egg slightly. Combine minced ingredients, egg and all of the remaining stuffing ingredients in a bowl and mix thoroughly. Fill the mushroom caps with stuffing, rounding off the tops. Garnish with coriander leaves. Boil water in lower section of your steamer. Line upper part with cheesecloth. Place stuffed mushroom caps in the steamer and steam, covered, for 15 minutes. Serve warm.

NOTE: Use one-third the amount of dried coriander if unable to find fresh coriander. Ground turkey used in place of the ground pork is good, too.

CLAM-STUFFED MUSHROOMS

2 lbs. large mushrooms
1 8-oz. can minced clams
1/2 cup butter
1 clove garlic, minced
1/2 cup dry bread crumbs
1/3 cup parsley, chopped
3/4 tsp. salt
1/4 tsp. pepper

Remove mushroom stems and place caps rounded side down on rack of broiler pan. Drain liquid from clams and reserve. In 10-inch skillet, over medium heat, melt butter and brush on caps. In remaining butter cook chopped stems, garlic and clam liquid for 5 minutes. Stir in clams and remaining ingredients. Spoon into caps and broil 8 minutes until tender.

NOTE: Very good variation on stuffed mushrooms. Add grated Parmesan cheese on top before broiling, if desired.

STUFFED MUSHROOMS

1-1/2 lbs. fresh broiler mushrooms
1 stick butter
1/2 tsp. garlic salt
4 Tbsp. bread crumbs
1/3 bunch Japanese spinach
4 Tbsp. shredded Cheddar cheese

Clean mushrooms by brushing with crumpled paper towel or napkin. Remove stems. Set aside caps. Dice stems and sauté in butter. Add seasoning, bread crumbs and spinach that has been chopped fine. Add Cheddar cheese and cook until cheese is about to melt. Remove from stove, fill mushroom caps with filling and broil in oven for 6-8 minutes on second rack from top until filling bubbles.

NOTE: This is an original recipe. People like it better than mushrooms stuffed with pork hash, etc.

MUSHROOMS STUFFED WITH CRABMEAT

24 large mushroom caps
1/2 cup melted butter
1-1/2 cups flaked crabmeat, fresh
2 eggs, lightly beaten
1/2 cup grated onion
3 Tbsp. mayonnaise
2 tsp. lemon juice
1/2 cup bread crumbs
1/2 cup grated Parmesan cheese

Preheat oven to 375°. Grease baking sheet. Dip clean mushroom caps in butter. Arrange on baking sheet, stem side up. In mixing bowl combine crabmeat, eggs, mayonnaise, onion, lemon juice and crumbs; mix lightly. Fill mushroom caps with crabmeat mixture. Sprinkle with cheese. Bake in preheated oven for 15 minutes.

CHICKEN-STUFFED MUSHROOMS

1 cup salad oil
1 Tbsp. finely chopped onion
1 Tbsp. finely chopped chives
2 tsp. finely chopped parsley
1 bay leaf
3 cloves
1/4 tsp. black pepper
Dash Tabasco sauce
1/2 tsp. salt
1 clove garlic, peeled, halved
1 lb. medium mushrooms, stems removed

Stuffing:
2 chicken breasts, cooked, finely minced
2-3 Tbsp. mayonnaise
3 Tbsp. chopped green onion
1/4 tsp. salt
2 Tbsp. sour cream

In large bowl combine oil, onion, chives, parsley, bay leaf, cloves, pepper, Tabasco, salt and garlic. Add mushrooms and marinate for 2 days, stirring occasionally. Mix together the chicken, mayonnaise, green onion, salt and sour cream to bind. Stuff mushrooms with chicken mixture and chill until ready to serve.

NOTE: This is one of my favorite recipes. People have a difficult time trying to decide what the stuffing is made of. They cannot believe it is chicken. You will love it. Here again, you can marinate the mushrooms in a plastic bag, vacuum sealing it by pushing out as much of the air as possible, and avoid having to stir occasionally. The marinade will completely surround the mushrooms. Do this when marinating meat, fish, etc. No need to stir or shake. All you need to do is occasionally turn the bag over.

MUSHROOM CROWNS

24-30 medium mushrooms
1 cup lean ground pork
4 medium prawns
6-8 water chestnuts, finely chopped
1 Tbsp. dark soy sauce
1 Tbsp. Sherry
1/2 tsp. salt
1/2 tsp. sugar
1 tsp. cornstarch
2 tsp. oil
1/2 cup chicken stock
4-5 Tbsp. oyster sauce
1 stalk green onion, chopped

Clean and stem mushrooms. Shell and devein prawns and mince them. Mix with water chestnuts, pork, soy sauce, Sherry, sugar, salt and cornstarch. Place about 1 teaspoonful of filling into each mushroom.

Heat 2 teaspoons of oil in skillet and place mushrooms in a single layer with the filling facing up. Brown for 1 minute. Pour 1/2 cup stock into skillet, cover and simmer for 8-10 minutes, adding more stock if necessary. Uncover. (There should be about 1/4 cup stock left in the skillet.) Add oyster sauce and baste the mushrooms. When sauce thickens, transfer to platter and garnish with chopped green onions.

SPINACH-STUFFED MUSHROOMS

1 lb. medium mushrooms
1 10-oz. pkg. frozen chopped spinach, squeezed dry
1 Tbsp. butter
2 Tbsp. flour
1/2 cup milk
Dash of salt
1/4 tsp. nutmeg
2 egg yolks
1/4 cup cooked, crumbled bacon
1/4 cup Parmesan cheese, grated

Clean mushrooms with mushroom brush or brush lightly with crumpled napkin or paper towel; remove stems. DO NOT WASH.

In small pan, melt butter; blend in flour with whisk. Whisking, add milk and seasoning. Cook until thickened.

Add yolks and remove from heat. Add spinach and bacon. Cool slightly and fill caps, mounding the tops slightly.

Dust with Parmesan cheese and bake at 350° for 10-15 minutes or until cheese is melted and tops are lightly browned.

NOTE: The egg yolks and bacon add a nice flavor to this delicious stuffed mushroom recipe.

MUSHROOMS STUFFED WITH SPINACH AND HAM

1/2 can cream of mushroom soup
1/2 tsp. salt
1/8 tsp. black pepper
Dash of nutmeg
1 10-oz. pkg. frozen spinach
2 Tbsp. butter
2 stalks scallions, finely chopped
1/4 cup cooked ham, finely diced
1 drop Tabasco sauce
1/4 tsp. Worcestershire sauce
24 large fresh mushroom caps, cleaned
Bread crumbs

Cook spinach according to package directions; cool under cold running water and remove all moisture by squeezing it in the palms of your hands. Finely chop the spinach. Melt butter, add scallions and ham and sauté for 3 minutes, stirring occasionally. Add spinach and cook for 3 minutes, stirring occasionally. Stir in the mushroom soup, salt, pepper, Tabasco and Worcestershire sauce. Season mushroom caps with salt and pepper and fill them with mixture. Sprinkle with bread crumbs, arrange on a greased baking pan, stuffed side up, and bake at 350° for 15 minutes. Serve immediately.

NOTE: The original recipe called for preparing a white sauce. The cream of mushroom soup works just as well, if not better, and it certainly cuts down on the work.

NUTTY STUFFED MUSHROOMS

24 medium mushrooms
2 Tbsp. butter
1 tsp. instant minced onion
1/2 cup dry bread crumbs
1/4 cup sliced almonds or Brazil nuts
2 strips crisp bacon, crumbled
1/4 tsp. salt
6 Tbsp. canned chicken broth

Clean mushrooms with mushroom brush or crumpled paper towel. DO NOT WASH. Remove stems and chop, reserving caps.

Heat butter and sauté stems for 2 minutes. Add onions and cook another 2 minutes. Combine stems and onion mixture in bowl with bread crumbs, nuts, bacon and salt. Add broth and mix well.

Stuff this mixture into the mushroom caps. Place in shallow, buttered dish and bake at 350° for 8-10 minutes or until heated through.

Variation: You may substitute pine nuts for the almonds or Brazil nuts.

NOTE: Mushrooms are very porous and will absorb water if they are washed. This will prevent them from absorbing any seasoning you may use. They will also get slimy if washed.

SNAILS IN MUSHROOM CAPS

1 stick butter
1 Tbsp. parsley, finely chopped
2 cloves garlic, finely diced
1 scallion, white part only, finely diced
1 tsp. seasoned salt
1 Tbsp. lemon juice
1/8 tsp. black pepper
12 large canned snails, drained and cut in half
24 fresh mushroom caps, 1-1/2 in. in diameter, cleaned

Blend together the butter, parsley, garlic, scallion, lemon juice and pepper. Place 1/4 teaspoon of garlic butter in each mushroom cap. Place one piece of snail in each mushroom cap.

Cover the snails with the remaining garlic butter and arrange caps on small dishes or in a baking dish lined with rock salt, which will hold the caps upright.

Broil 4 inches away from the broiling element for 4-6 minutes. The caps are ready when the butter is golden brown.

Serve hot.

NOTE: Even people with an aversion to snails will love this. Have lots of napkins ready to wipe the butter that drips from their mouths.

MUSHROOM NEWBURG

1/4 cup butter
1 lb. mushrooms, cleaned and halved
2 Tbsp. flour
1-1/4 cups milk or half-and-half
1/4 cup dry sherry
1/4 tsp. salt
1/8 tsp. ground nutmeg
3 egg yolks, beaten
4 frozen patty shells, prepared according to package directions

Melt butter in saucepan. Add mushrooms and sauté for 5 minutes. Remove with slotted spoon and reserve.

Mix flour with melted butter. Slowly add milk and Sherry, stirring constantly, until smooth sauce is formed. Stir in salt and nutmeg; simmer gently for 10 minutes. Mix 3 tablespoons of this sauce into egg yolks; stir egg yolk mixture into the sauce. Add reserved mushrooms. Taste and adjust seasonings.

Cook for about 2 minutes, stirring constantly until mixture bubbles. Spoon mushroom sauce into patty shells and serve.

NOTE: In place of the patty shells use the Mini Shrimp Tartlets pastry, page 16. Tartlets can be done ahead, frozen, thawed to room temperature, filled with stuffing, warmed and served.

MUSHROOM MINI-CORNUCOPIA

Pastry Crust:
2 cups all-purpose flour
3/4 tsp. salt
2/3 cup shortening
4-5 Tbsp. cold or ice water

Sift flour and salt into mixing bowl. Cut shortening in to resemble fine crumbs. Sprinkle water over the surface and mix together lightly. Gather into a ball and roll out on lightly floured pastry board to 1/8-inch thickness. Using a lightly floured 1-1/2-inch-diameter drinking glass, cut out pastry rounds.

Filling:
2 Tbsp. butter
1 small onion, chopped fine
1/2 lb. fresh mushrooms, cleaned and chopped fine
Dash cayenne pepper
3 Tbsp. sour cream
1 hard boiled egg, chopped fine
1 Tbsp. cooked rice
1/4 tsp. salt
1/8 tsp. black pepper
1 egg yolk, slightly beaten
1 Tbsp. cream

Melt butter in skillet. Add onions and mushrooms. Sauté 5 minutes until onions are transparent. Transfer onion mixture to mixing bowl. Add egg, rice, salt, black and cayenne pepper and sour cream. Blend thoroughly.

Place 1/2 teaspoon filling on center of each pastry round. Moisten two-thirds of outer edge of the rounds with water. Bring moistened edges together. Pinch, tapering the end to form a horn shape. Fold back the opposite end and leave it open. Place filled pastry horns on baking sheet. Brush with mixture of egg yolk and cream. Bake at 400° for 10-15 minutes until lightly browned.

FRENCH FRIED MUSHROOMS

1/3 cup flour
1/4 cup dry bread crumbs
1-1/2 tsp. salt
1/4 tsp. white pepper
1/4 tsp. thyme
1/4 tsp. rosemary
1/2 tsp. oregano
1 lb. fresh mushrooms (medium whole or large quartered), cleaned
1 egg, lightly beaten

In mixing bowl combine flour, bread crumbs, salt, pepper, thyme, rosemary and oregano. Dip mushrooms into beaten egg. With slotted spoon remove mushrooms to flour mixture. Toss well to coat. Fry in deep hot oil until golden brown. Drain on paper towels and serve hot.

NOTE: This will replace french fried potatoes in your family.

CRISPY MUSHROOM CHIPS

Nonstick cooking spray
1/2 lb. large mushrooms

Preheat oven to 250°. Coat large baking sheet with cooking spray and set aside. Using sharp knife, slice the mushrooms very thin, then transfer to the baking sheet, arranging the slices in a single layer. Bake uncovered for 2 to 2-1/2 hours or until crisp and completely dry.

NOTE: Check often to see that they are not overdone. You will find that mushrooms, without any seasoning, have a very distinct taste that grows on you.

ITALIAN MUSHROOMS

1/2 lb. fresh mushrooms or 3 4-oz. cans mushrooms, drained
1/4 cup water or mushroom liquid
1/2 cup Wishbone Italian Dressing

If using fresh mushrooms, clean thoroughly with mushroom brush or crumpled paper towel and trim 1/4 inch from the stem. Place in a Ziplock plastic bag with 1/4 cup water and bottled dressing.

If using canned mushrooms, drain, reserve liquid. Place in a Ziplock plastic bag with 1/4 cup of the mushroom liquid and bottled dressing.

Remove all the air from the bag so marinade will completely surround the mushrooms. Refrigerate overnight and enjoy.

You may add or decrease liquid according to your taste. Shake dressing well before mixing with the mushrooms.

NOTE: I first tasted this on the mainland at the Kurata's and almost devoured a whole quart of huge, fresh marinated mushrooms. I never forgot how good they were and learned how easy they are to prepare. If you are a mushroom lover, this will become your favorite recipe.

ORIENTAL FRESH MUSHROOMS

16 fresh mushrooms,
    1 to 1-1/2 in. in diameter
Lemon juice
1/2 lb. ground pork
1/4 cup minced water chestnuts
1/4 cup untoasted sesame seeds

1 egg, slightly beaten
1 tsp. soy sauce
1/4 tsp. garlic powder
1/4 lb. butter, melted
1/4 cup minced green onions

Preheat oven to 350°. Clean mushrooms; remove and reserve stems. If preparing in advance, rub with lemon juice. Chop mushroom stems finely and combine with pork, water chestnuts, green onion, egg, soy sauce and garlic powder. Stuff caps with mixture and coat cap bottoms with butter. Top with sesame seeds. Put in large baking dish and bake for 30-40 minutes. Serve immediately.

JUANITA'S MARINATED MUSHROOMS

1/2 cup salad oil	1/2 tsp. salt
1/3 cup cider vinegar	2 tsp. sugar
2 Tbsp. green onion, chopped	20 small mushrooms, sliced
2 Tbsp. parsley, chopped	1 round onion, sliced thin
1 clove garlic, minced	2 cucumbers, seeded and sliced thin

Make marinade with oil, vinegar, green onion, parsley, garlic and seasonings. Add sliced mushrooms, onion and cucumbers and marinate 4 hours or overnight.

Serve with some of the marinade in a nice bowl.

NOTE: The cucumbers are completely different from the mushrooms both in texture and taste. You will like this dish and find it an instant hit.

You may add more mushrooms, onion and cucumbers to remaining marinade and have another supply of these delicious marinated mushrooms.

MUSHROOMS WITH RAISINS

1 Tbsp. butter
1/2 lb. mushrooms, cleaned, stems removed
3 oz. dry white wine
3 oz. catsup
2 oz. raisins

Melt butter in saucepan. Add mushrooms and gently sauté over moderate heat for 2 minutes, stirring constantly.

Add wine, catsup and raisins; simmer for 1 minute.

Pour mixture into a bowl and chill until ready to serve. Drain and serve on a bed of lettuce.

NOTE: The raisins in this recipe add a slightly sweet flavor.

MARINATED MUSHROOMS

25 fresh mushrooms
1 hard-cooked egg yolk, mashed
1/3 cup wine vinegar
1/3 cup vegetable oil
1/2 tsp. salt
1/2 tsp. white pepper
2 tsp. chopped parsley
1 tsp. Dijon mustard
1 Tbsp. brown sugar

Mix together all ingredients except mushrooms. Bring to a boil and add cleaned mushrooms. Cook 5 to 6 minutes. Cool and refrigerate overnight in the marinade. Serve with toothpicks.

VEGETABLES

CUCUMBER CHICKEN RINGS

2 cucumbers
1 large chicken breast, cooked, boned, and minced
1 hard boiled egg, finely chopped
2 Tbsp. chopped fresh parsley
Salt and pepper to taste
2-3 Tbsp. mayonnaise
Fresh bread
Parsley for garnish

Remove strips of skin from cucumber and cut into thirds. Remove seed, leaving a hole in the center.

Mix minced chicken, chopped egg, parsley, salt and pepper and mayonnaise. Stuff cucumber with this mixture. Wrap in plastic wrap and chill 2-3 hours.

Using a cookie cutter, cut 26 rounds of bread and spread with mayonnaise. Slice cucumbers into 1/4-inch slices and place on bread rounds. Serve.

NOTE: If you like crisp cucumbers, soak in ice water for 30 minutes, drain well and stuff. Leftover stuffed cucumbers will get soggy, so assemble only what you will need for one sitting. Make more as you need them. Top a few slices with a dash of paprika for color.

CUCUMBER AND WALNUT MISO

2/3 cup walnuts
1/2 cup red miso
1/4 cup sugar
1/4 cup mirin
2 Tbsp. rice wine
1 English cucumber

Mince walnuts. In saucepan combine miso, sugar, mirin and rice wine. Cook over low heat while stirring constantly for 5 minutes.

Remove from heat and stir in walnuts. Set aside to cool.

Cut cucumbers into 3-inch sections and core. Then cut each section into 1-inch sections and quarter each section. Spoon a little miso and walnut mixture on each section and serve.

NOTE: I would never have dreamed of combining miso and walnuts—not in a million years—and yet, here is a great recipe. Try it and I know you will be pleased and excited about this. It was the hit of our latest New Year's Eve party.

Cucumbers will get soggy if left sitting, so fill only what you need for one sitting.

VEGETABLES

SOUR CREAM AND CUCUMBERS

2 cucumbers, peeled and thinly sliced
1 small onion, thinly sliced
1/3-1/2 cup distilled vinegar
Salt and pepper to taste
2 Tbsp. sugar
8 oz. sour cream

Place cucumbers and onions in shallow dish. Cover with vinegar, salt, pepper and sugar. Chill overnight. Next day, drain well, mix in sour cream and adjust taste. Chill until ready to serve.

SWEET AND SOUR CUCUMBER PICKLES

4 large cucumbers
1/2 cup sugar
1/2 cup rice vinegar
1/2 cup shoyu

Peel cucumbers, leaving some strips of green, and slice about 1/8 inch thick. Pour sugar, vinegar and shoyu over the cucumbers and mix gently until sugar is dissolved. Leave in refrigerator 30 minutes or more. Stir before serving.

NOTE: This is good as a vegetable dish for your family also. Can be kept in the refrigerator for a few days.

RAW CUCUMBER AND COOKED CRAB

1/2 lb. fresh frozen crabmeat
2 Tbsp. rice vinegar
2 tsp. sugar
1 tsp. shoyu
Dash of salt
Dash of pepper
4 cucumbers

Peel cucumbers, leaving some strips of green, and slice into 1/2 to 3/4-inch-thick slices. Spoon out the seeds, leaving a thin layer on the bottom. Blend crabmeat with remaining ingredients and spoon a teaspoon of it onto the cucumber. Serve cold.

NOTE: Soak the cucumber in water with ice for about 10 minutes to keep it crisp in the refrigerator. Drain well and fill. Do this just before serving, since the cucumber lets off water and will dilute the flavor of the crab mix.

SHIOFUKE KONBU CUCUMBER

1 long cucumber
1.4-oz. pkg. shiofuke konbu

Cut cucumber lengthwise in half and remove seeds. Slice approximately 1/8-inch thick and sprinkle shiofuke konbu on top. Mix well. Let stand about 15 minutes before serving.

NOTE: The long European variety of cucumber stays crisp longer. The salt and shoyu flavor from the konbu (seaweed) gives the cucumber a very nice taste.

OCCIDENTAL NAMASU

3 large cucumbers
3 medium cauliflower
2 medium daikon (white radish)
4 medium carrots
8-10 stalks celery
4 large sweet onions
2 cups sugar
1-1/2 cups water
1 cup distilled vinegar
1/4 cup Hawaiian (rock) salt

Cut cucumbers into 2-1/2-inch julienne strips, leaving skin but removing seeds. Do the same with the daikon, carrots and celery. Cut cauliflower into bite-sized pieces. Cut each onion into 8 quarters.

Mix remaining ingredients and pour over cut vegetables in a large bowl. Mix well, cover with plastic wrap to keep it from drying out, and refrigerate for 2 days, turning frequently. Yields about 2 gallons.

NOTE: Don't worry that the sauce doesn't cover the vegetables. Water will come out of the vegetables as they marinate. This recipe makes a large quantity and is good for receptions and fundraisers. Do not use an aluminum bowl when marinating the vegetables.

DAY-AHEAD VEGETABLES

4 oz. Hidden Valley Ranch original salad dressing mix
1 cup mayonnaise
1 cup sour cream
2 green onions, green parts only chopped
1 lb. bite-sized broccoli flowerets
1 lb. bite-sized cauliflower flowerets
3 carrots, peeled, sliced 1/4 in. thick

The day before serving, prepare vegetables. With wire whisk mix dressing mix with sour cream and mayonnaise. Add chopped green onions and pour over vegetables. Place in Ziplock plastic bag, remove all the air, and marinate overnight, turning occasionally.

EGG ROLLS WITH PEANUT BUTTER

1-1/2 cups bean sprouts
1 cup cooked shrimp, diced
1 cup cooked beef, minced, or raw ground beef
1 cup celery, minced
1 cup green onion, finely minced
1 6-1/2-oz. can water chestnuts, drained and diced
1 Tbsp. oil
4 Tbsp. creamy peanut butter
1-1/2 tsp. salt
1-1/2 tsp. sugar
1/8 tsp. ground black pepper
1/4 tsp. Chinese Five Spice powder
20-21 egg roll wrappers

Mix all ingredients except egg roll wrappers.

Place 2-3 teaspoons of mixture in center of egg roll wrappers. Fold both sides toward the center and roll. Moisten end to seal. Fry in lots of hot oil until golden brown in color.

Serve with hot mustard mixed with shoyu or a sweet and sour sauce for dipping.

NOTE: The peanut butter gives a nice, different flavor to an otherwise ordinary egg roll. Add more if you are partial to peanut butter.

VEGETABLE MOCHI FRY

2 Tbsp. sugar
2 Tbsp. shoyu
1 pkg. hondashi (Oriental seasoning)
Julienne strips of string beans, carrots and shiitake mushrooms,
    soaked in water to soften
Bacon
Mochi squares

Cook vegetables in sugar, shoyu, hondashi, and shiitake water until carrots are no longer crunchy but not falling apart. Cut mochi squares into thirds. To each piece of mochi add one of each vegetable and roll with 1/2 strip of bacon. Fasten with toothpick, roll in cornstarch and fry in about 1/2 inch of hot oil.

NOTE: This recipe came from a 4-H recipe contest as a main dish. It is very good as a pupu—unusual and tasty.

SHRIMP VEGETABLE TEMPURA

2 cups flour
1/4 cup cornstarch
2 Tbsp. sugar, heaping
2 Tbsp. salt
1 Tbsp. baking powder
1-1/2 cups mixture of evaporated milk and water
1/2 lb. fresh shrimp, chopped
Carrots, beans, parsley, cut in fine julienne strips

Mix flour, cornstarch, sugar, salt and baking powder and add milk slowly, to prevent lumps. Add remaining ingredients and mix well to coat completely. Drop by tablespoons into hot oil and cook until slightly brown.

NOTE: This recipe can be used for French Fried Onion Rings also. They're delicious—the kids will love them.

LUMPIA WITH LETTUCE

6 oz. cooked frozen baby shrimp, thawed
1 Tbsp. vegetable oil
1/4 lb. fresh pork sausage
1 clove garlic, minced
1 medium onion, diced
2 cups Chinese cabbage, minced
1 cup fresh bean sprouts
1/4 tsp. salt
1/4 tsp. black pepper
20-24 firm lettuce leaves
Slightly Sour Apricot Sauce

Drain shrimp; set aside. Heat oil in large skillet. Add sausage, garlic and onion, and sauté 10 minutes until sausage is completely cooked. Add Chinese cabbage, bean sprouts, salt and pepper. Cook 3-5 minutes until vegetables are tender-crisp. Stir in shrimp and heat through. Keep warm. Wash lettuce and pat dry. Steam for 30 seconds, then arrange leaves on large serving platter. Divide mixture among leaves, bring sides of each leaf to center, and then roll up. Place seam side down and serve warm or at room temperature with Slightly Sour Apricot Sauce.

SLIGHTLY SOUR APRICOT SAUCE

1/2 cup apricot preserves
1/4 cup white wine vinegar
1 tsp. minced ginger
1 Tbsp. honey

Combine above in small saucepan; bring to a boil. Cool and serve.

SWEET AND SOUR BROCCOLI

1 lb. broccoli stems
2 Tbsp. white vinegar
2 Tbsp. sugar
1 tsp. salt
2 Tbsp. sesame seed oil

Peel broccoli stems and cut into diagonal slices 1/8-inch to 1/6-inch thick. Combine vinegar, sugar, oil and salt in large jar. Add the broccoli and shake to coat well. Cover and refrigerate overnight, shaking occasionally. Drain and place in serving dish. Serve with toothpicks.

NOTE: You may use the flowerets in the same manner. They will absorb the marinade faster, so you may want to add them to the marinade later than the stems. I would suggest marinating them in a separate jar. A plastic bag sealed tightly will work also.

EGGPLANT PICKLES

6 medium Japanese eggplants
1/2 cup sugar
1/2 cup shoyu
1/4 cup rice vinegar
2 Tbsp. rock salt

Slice eggplant about 1/8 inch thick and sprinkle with rock salt. Let it sit for 2 hours; then gently squeeze some of the liquid out. Combine remaining ingredients and add to eggplant. Stir well, place in containers and refrigerate.

NOTE: This can be eaten immediately and keeps for two weeks in the refrigerator.

SAUERKRAUT BALLS

1/2 lb. pork sausage, finely crumbled
1/4 cup onion, finely chopped
1 14-oz. can sauerkraut, drained and chopped
2 Tbsp. bread crumbs
3 oz. cream cheese
2 Tbsp. parsley, chopped
1 tsp. prepared mustard
1/4 tsp. garlic salt
1/8 tsp. pepper
1/4 cup flour
1 egg, well beaten
1/4 cup milk
3/4 cup bread crumbs

In medium frying pan, brown sausage and onions. Drain fat and add sauerkraut and 2 tablespoons bread crumbs. Combine cream cheese, parsley, mustard, garlic salt and pepper and stir into meat mixture and chill for 2 hours. Shape into small balls and coat with flour. Dip into mixture of egg and milk and then into bread crumbs. Fry in hot oil until lightly browned, about 3-5 minutes.

NOTE: This may be prepared a day ahead, refrigerated and warmed in the oven before serving. Will keep well in the refrigerator for several days. I love sauerkraut, so I was happy to find this pupu recipe.

MUSTARD CABBAGE KIM CHEE

1 head mustard cabbage
1 Tbsp. rock salt
1/2 small round onion
3 Tbsp. Momoya kim chee base
3 Tbsp. shoyu

Wash mustard cabbage leaves and cut into 2-inch pieces. Add salt. Mix slightly and let stand 15-20 minutes. Place a handful of the salted leaves in a muslin dishcloth and wring out as much of the liquid as possible. Add chopped onion, kim chee base and shoyu. Mix well and refrigerate.

NOTE: Very good as a side dish also. May be made with less kim chee base. Keeps in refrigerator for a long time.

TAKO KIM CHEE

1/2 bottle kim chee
1 pkg. frozen tako, thawed

Chop kim chee into bite-sized pieces and mix with frozen tako that has also been sliced into bite-sized pieces. Add some kim chee juice and let stand 2-3 hours before serving.

KOREAN OGO (SEAWEED)

2 lbs. ogo (seaweed)
1/2 cup rice vinegar
3/4 cup shoyu
1/3 cup sugar
1 tsp. hot sauce
6 stalks green onion, chopped
1 small onion, sliced thin
1/2 tsp. grated ginger
1 clove garlic, grated
2 Tbsp. dried shrimp, chopped
1 small Hawaiian chili pepper, seeded and chopped

Clean and wash ogo. Boil water in a medium saucepan and add ogo. Stir briskly for a few seconds until ogo turns green.

Pour into a colander and rinse under running water to stop cooking process. Drain.

Make marinade with remaining ingredients. Add chopped drained ogo and mix well. Taste; add more seasoning if desired. Marinate in the refrigerator overnight and serve.

NOTE: This recipe makes enough sauce to amply marinate 2 pounds of ogo. I changed the quantities of the ingredients from the original recipe I found in a local cookbook many years ago. It is always a hit, no matter how many times I serve it.

KOREAN WARABE

1/2 bottle Okura sushi vinegar
2 Tbsp. sesame oil
1 Tbsp. sesame seed
2 Tbsp. Koo Choo Jung sauce
1/4 cup dried shrimp, chopped
1/4 cup green onion, chopped
2 lbs. warabe (fern shoot)

Clean warabe and cut into 1-inch lengths. Blanch in boiling water, drain and immediately pour cold water over to stop the cooking process. Make a marinade out of the remaining ingredients and mix well with warabe. Refrigerate.

KONBU KAKUMA KIMPIRA

1 pkg. kizami or kiri konbu (seaweed)
6 cups slivered kakuma (fern shoot)
3 pkgs. dashinomoto (Oriental seasoning)
1/4 cup shoyu
1/4 cup sugar
1/4 cup mirin
1/2 tsp. salt
1/2 tsp. pepper flakes

Soak konbu in hot tap water for 20 minutes; drain. Fry kakuma in hot oil with handful of dried shrimp and a little salt. Add seasonings and seaweed and cook on medium-low heat until liquid is reduced to about 1/3, stirring occasionally every 15-20 minutes.

NOTE: Very economical and a good way to use kakuma when in season. Changing the water in which the kakuma is soaking in the refrigerator every few days will keep the kakuma indefinitely in the refrigerator.

SHIOFUKE KONBU WARABE

1 to 1-1/2 lbs. warabe (fern shoot)
1 1.5-oz. pkg. shiofuke konbu (salted seaweed slivers), chopped
1 kamaboko, slivered
1 small round onion, sliced thin
Handful dried shrimp, chopped
1/2-1 tsp. sesame oil

Clean warabe in water, washing off all the hair, dirt, etc. Break off woody, brittle ends. Cut into 1-1/2-inch pieces. Boil a large pot of water. Have a large bowl of water with ice sitting on the side. Place cut warabe in boiling water; stir and blanch for about 30 seconds or until warabe turns bright green. Drain immediately and place warabe in bowl of ice water to stop cooking process. Drain warabe when ice has completely melted. Place warabe in bowl with shiofuke konbu, sliced onions, chopped shrimp, slivered kamaboko and sesame oil. Mix well and refrigerate for an hour or two until ready to eat.

NOTE: The secret to the crunchiness of this recipe is the ice-water bath. For variation mix cooked warabe with sliced tomatoes and use namasu sauce as a marinade. I've also enjoyed warabe with chopped, salted salmon as the only source of seasoning with some chopped round onion. It was very delicious and refreshing. Good as a salad or vegetable dish.

VEGETABLES

VEGETABLES

SWEET AND SOUR MARINATED ONIONS

3-1/2 Tbsp. olive oil
1 small onion, chopped
1 clove garlic, minced
1 medium tomato, skinned and chopped
1 sprig parsley
1 bay leaf
1/4 tsp. basil
1/4 tsp. thyme
1/2 tsp. salt
White pepper to taste
1/2 lb. pearl onions, 1-1/2 inches in diameter, peeled
1/4 cup white wine vinegar
2 Tbsp. raisins
2 tsp. sugar

Heat 2 tablespoons oil in small skillet and sauté chopped onion and garlic until onion is wilted. Add tomato, sauté for a minute, then add the parsley, bay leaf, 1/8 teaspoon of basil and thyme, salt, pepper and 2 tablespoons of water. Cover and simmer for 20 minutes. Place the pearl onions in a saucepan with 1/2 cup water, vinegar, the remaining 1-1/2 tablespoons of oil, the tomato mixture, the remaining 1/8 teaspoon of basil and thyme, the raisins, salt, pepper and sugar. Bring to a boil, reduce to a simmer and cook uncovered for 45 minutes. Cool and refrigerate. The onions will keep for many days in the refrigerator.

NOTE: Using only onions as a pupu is unusual, but you will enjoy this once you try it.

GREEN ONION MISO

1 bunch skinny-leaf green onion
Boiling water
3/4 cup miso
2 Tbsp. sugar
1 Tbsp. rice vinegar
2 Tbsp. wine

Clean green onion well, cutting off roots. Blanch in boiling water and rinse off immediately to stop cooking process. Mix miso, sugar, vinegar, and wine to make a sauce. Refrigerate. Take green onion stalks and tie each into a loop and fasten by rolling the green onion around the center and securing by pulling the end back through the loop. Dip in chilled miso sauce and enjoy.

NOTE: Boiling takes the bitterness out of the green onion. There is a pleasant release of air in the mouth when you bite down into it. I used to enjoy this as a child. It must be old Japanese country cooking.

FRIED ONION RINGS

2 cups flour
1/4 cup cornstarch
2 heaping Tbsp. sugar
2 tsp. salt
1 Tbsp. baking powder
1-1/2 cups evaporated milk or water
Sliced onion rings

Mix first six ingredients well to prevent lumps. Add onion rings, a few at a time, and deep fry in hot oil. Drain and serve.

SPINACH QUICHE SQUARES

1 cup milk
1 cup flour
3 eggs, beaten
1/2 tsp. baking powder
1 clove garlic, finely chopped
1 lb. Monterey Jack cheese, shredded
4 10-oz. pkgs. frozen spinach, thawed and drained
1/4 cup butter

In a large bowl mix well the first 5 ingredients. Add cheese and spinach. Melt the butter in a 9- x 12-inch baking pan while oven is preheating to 350°, approximately 3-4 minutes. Pour spinach mixture into pan, filling all corners.

Bake at 350° for 30 minutes or until edges are browned. Cool completely and cut into 1-1/2-inch squares. You can quick-freeze them at this point, drop them into a plastic bag and store in the freezer.

To serve, heat in 350° oven for 15 minutes without defrosting.

SPINACH TORTILLA ROLL

2 10-oz. pkgs. frozen chopped spinach, drained
1 2-oz. pkg. Hidden Valley Ranch dressing mix
8 oz. sour cream
1 cup mayonnaise
1/2 of 3.4-oz. bottle bacon bits
1/4 cup water chestnuts, chopped
6 stalks green onion, chopped
8 flour tortillas

Thaw and drain frozen spinach, squeeze out excess liquid and chop fine. Add remaining ingredients and mix well.

Place 1/3 cup of mixture on a tortilla and spread evenly over the entire surface. Roll as you would sushi and set aside, seam side down, until you have finished rolling all the spinach mixture.

Chill until time to serve. Cut into 1/4-inch slices and serve.

NOTE: I have used this as a sandwich spread on whole wheat bread and have had people rave about it. It is especially nice double-deckered and cut into tea-size sandwiches. I have also used this as a vegetable dip, using more mayonnaise to make it more dippable.

SPINACH BALLS

1/2 cup butter
2 large onions, chopped
2 boxes frozen chopped spinach
6 eggs
1 tsp. seasoned salt
2 cups Pepperidge Farm herb stuffing
1 cup grated Parmesan cheese
1/2 tsp. thyme
1 tsp. pepper
1 tsp. garlic salt

Melt butter in skillet and sauté onions. Defrost and squeeze spinach dry. Add to onion and cook 1-2 minutes. Combine eggs, seasoned salt, stuffing, cheese and seasonings. Add spinach mixture. Shape into 1-inch balls. Place on foil-lined cookie sheet and bake at 350° for 20 minutes until golden.

NOTE: Spinach balls may be frozen on cookie sheets, then wrapped airtight.

MARINATED SLICED TOMATOES

3 Tbsp. salad oil
1-1/2 Tbsp. cider vinegar
1 Tbsp. minced parsley
3/4 tsp. garlic salt
1 tsp. sugar
1/8 tsp. oregano
Dash pepper
2 firm medium tomatoes

In cup or small bowl, combine all dressing ingredients; stir with wire whisk or fork until well blended. With sharp knife, thinly slice tomatoes and arrange on a plate. Pour dressing over tomatoes, cover with plastic wrap and refrigerate at least 1 hour to blend flavors.

NOTE: About 115 calories per serving, serves 4. If you use tomato wedges, marinate a little longer.

STUFFED CHERRY TOMATOES

20-25 cherry tomatoes
3/4 cup pitted, imported oil-cured olives
4 anchovy fillets
1 clove garlic
2 Tbsp. well-drained capers
1 Tbsp. fresh basil, chopped
1 Tbsp. fresh parsley, chopped
1 Tbsp. lemon juice
3 Tbsp. olive oil

Cut tops off cherry tomatoes. Seed and turn upside down on a paper-towel-lined plate. Coarsely chop olives and set aside. Rinse anchovies in cold water and pat dry.

In blender or processor with steel blade, combine olives, anchovies, garlic, capers, basil, parsley and lemon juice. Process until finely minced. Slowly add olive oil. Remove mixture to a bowl and stir well.

Pack each cherry tomato with about 1-1/2 teaspoons of olive mixture. Set on parsley- or lettuce-lined plate. Serve at room temperature.

NOTE: Do not freeze. Fill tomatoes an hour before serving. Filling may be made a day or more ahead and kept refrigerated. Bring to room temperature before serving. This has an exotic taste and is very delicious. Wash anchovy well as it is very salty.

ARTICHOKE NIBBLES

2 jars marinated artichoke hearts
1 small onion, finely minced
1 clove garlic, finely minced
4 eggs
1/4 cup fine bread crumbs
1/4 tsp. salt
1/8 tsp. each pepper, oregano, Tabasco
1/2 lb. shredded sharp Cheddar cheese
2 Tbsp. minced parsley

Drain marinade from one jar of artichokes into a frying pan. Add onion, garlic and chopped artichoke hearts and sauté until onion is limp, about 5 minutes. In bowl beat eggs with fork, and add crumbs, salt, pepper, oregano and Tabasco. Stir in cheese, parley and artichoke-onion mixture. Turn into greased 7- x 11-inch baking pan and bake at 325° for 30 minutes or until set. Let cool in pan; then cut into 1-inch pieces.

NOTE: This tastes best when it is warm. Even people who do not normally like artichokes like this.

ZUCCHINI PUFFS

2 cups flour
1 tsp. baking powder
1 egg
2 Tbsp. olive oil
1-1/4 cups milk
1/2 tsp. salt
1/4 tsp. white pepper
1-1/2 cups grated Cheddar cheese
2 medium zucchini, grated and drained in colander
2 cloves garlic, grated
2 Tbsp. finely chopped onion
1 Tbsp. minced parsley
Oil for frying
Salt to taste

Sift flour and baking powder; set aside. In large bowl combine egg, olive oil, 1/2 cup milk, salt and pepper. Beat to smooth paste and gradually add sifted flour mixture. Consistency will be very stiff. Add grated cheese and remaining milk to make smooth but stiff batter. Blend in grated zucchini, garlic, onion and parsley. Heat oil and drop batter by spoonfuls. Fry until golden. Remove with slotted spoon and drain on paper towels. Keep warm until all batter is cooked. Lightly salt to taste and serve immediately.

NOTE: Your guests will love these. The flavor is subtle and you may find there is no need to salt them further before serving.

ZUCCHINI STICKS

1 quart water
1/4 cup rock salt
3 zucchini, cut in 2-inch julienne strips
2 eggs
1/2 cup water
Bread crumbs

Soak julienne strips of zucchini in salt water in refrigerator for 20 to 30 minutes. Wipe strips dry and dip in bread crumbs, then water and egg mixture and back into bread crumbs again. Deep fry until golden brown.

NOTE: This is well worth the time spent in frying. It will be gone as soon as you put the plate down.

CHICKEN

BUTTERED-HONEY CHICKEN BITS

4 chicken breasts, boned
4 Tbsp. butter
4 Tbsp. honey
2 tsp. teriyaki sauce
1 tsp. salt
1/2 tsp. garlic salt
1/4 tsp. pepper
1/2 cup sesame seeds

Melt butter and honey in small saucepan. Add teriyaki sauce.

Sprinkle bite-sized pieces of chicken breast with salt, garlic salt and pepper.

Dip each piece into honey, butter and teriyaki sauce mixture and roll in sesame seeds.

Place chicken pieces on baking sheet. Bake at 350° for about 30 minutes, turning once to brown evenly. Reheat remaining sauce to serve with cooked pieces of chicken.

NOTE: Mix 1 Tbsp. cornstarch and 1/4 cup water. Add just enough of this mixture to remaining sauce to thicken and use as a dip.

Freezes well. The sesame seeds will fall off, but just pile them on again when reheating in the oven before serving.

CHICKEN, MUSHROOM, AND WATER CHESTNUT SKEWERS

2 lbs. chicken breasts, boned
1/2 cup shoyu
1/2 cup dry white wine
1/2 tsp. dry mustard
Pepper to taste
2 Tbsp. chopped parsley
1 medium onion, chopped into large cubes
1/4 cup peanut oil
Several slices fresh ginger root
1 small can whole mushrooms
1 can water chestnuts

Cut chicken breasts along grain into 3-4 strips; cut into bite-sized cubes. Combine shoyu, wine, mustard, pepper, parsley, onion, oil and ginger for marinade. Add chicken pieces, mushrooms and water chestnuts and marinate one hour at room temperature or 24 hours in the refrigerator. Place chicken, mushrooms, water chestnuts and onions on 6-inch skewers that have been soaked in water to prevent burning. Broil for 3 minutes per side; do not overcook. Chicken should be lightly browned and juicy inside.

NOTE: Two pounds of chicken breasts makes about 60 skewers, depending on how many pieces of chicken, etc., you wish to place on them. Delicious and very popular. Your friends will ask for repeat performances.

PICKLED CUCUMBER AND CHICKEN

5 medium cucumbers	2 Tbsp. white sesame seeds
2 lbs. chicken thighs	2 cloves garlic, grated
5 Tbsp. sugar	2-3 chili peppers, chopped
1/2 cup distilled vinegar	Green onion, minced
1/2 cup shoyu	Parsley (optional)
1 tsp. sesame oil	

The night before, cut cucumbers into 1/2-inch by 1-1/4-inch lengthwise slices and soak in ice water for 20 minutes to crisp. Boil chicken thighs in salted water for about 20 minutes. Bone, shred and chop chicken into 1-inch pieces. Drain cucumbers. Mix remaining ingredients for marinade; add cucumbers and chicken. Chill until time to serve.

NOTE: Remove all fat from chicken before mixing with cucumbers and marinade. Just before serving, remove all fat that may be floating in the marinade.

FRIED CHICKEN WITH NORI

2 lbs. chicken breasts	Marinade:
2 sheets nori	1/4 cup shoyu
1/2 cup cornstarch	2 tsp. sugar
	1 tsp. sake

Bone chicken breasts, remove skin and slice breasts into three or four strips. Cut those strips into 1-1/2-inch pieces and marinate. Let stand 20-30 minutes. Cut nori into thirds and then into 1/2-inch pieces. Roll marinated chicken pieces in cornstarch and bind each with a piece of nori around the center, securing the nori by moistening with the marinade liquid. Fry in deep hot oil until nicely brown and crisp.

NOTE: When using 5 lbs. of chicken breasts, double the marinade recipe.

MACADAMIA CHICKEN STRIPS

2 cups flour
1 to 2 tsp. salt, depending on saltiness of nuts
12 oz. roasted macadamia nuts, finely chopped
1 lb. chicken, boned, cut in strips 3/4 x 3 inches long
1/2 cup butter, melted
4 eggs, lightly beaten

Preheat oven to 350°. Pour flour and salt into a plastic bag. Place nuts into another plastic bag. Taking a small handful at a time, dip chicken strips in melted butter to coat, then put in flour-filled bag. Shake to coat and shake off excess flour. Dip in beaten eggs. Shake off excess egg and place in macadamia-nut-filled bag. Shake to coat. Place chicken strips on ungreased, nonstick cookie sheet and bake 20 minutes.

NOTE: Store in refrigerator in an airtight container if done ahead. Serve at room temperature.

This can also be frozen. Thaw and serve at room temperature or warm in oven before serving.

I love pecans, so I sometimes use chopped pecans in place of the macadamia nuts.

SPINACH-WRAPPED CHICKEN WITH ORIENTAL DIP

2 lbs. chicken breasts
1 14-oz. can chicken broth
1/4 cup shoyu
1 Tbsp. Pickapeppa
1 lb. fresh spinach
Oriental Dip

Place chicken breasts, broth, shoyu and Pickapeppa in pan and bring to a boil. Simmer 15-20 minutes until fork tender. Lift chicken from broth. Cool. Remove and discard skin and bones. Cut meat into 1-inch chunks. Wash spinach, remove and discard stems and parboil. Drain thoroughly; set aside to cool. Place chunk of chicken at stem end of a large spinach leaf. Roll over once, fold leaf in toward center on both sides and continue rolling. Secure with toothpick. Refrigerate finished spinach rolls until thoroughly chilled or until the next day. Serve cold with Oriental Dip. Yield: 50-60 pieces.

ORIENTAL DIP

Stir together 1/2 cup sour cream, 1 tsp. toasted sesame seeds, 1/4 tsp. ground ginger, 2 tsp. shoyu, and 1 tsp. Worcestershire sauce until blended. Refrigerate until chilled or until the next day.

MINI CHICKEN-FILO ROLLS

1 chicken breast, finely minced
8 water chestnuts, finely minced
1 4-oz. can mushrooms, finely minced
2 stalks green onion, finely minced
1 Tbsp. cornstarch
1 tsp. sesame oil
1 tsp. light shoyu
1/2 tsp. distilled vinegar
1/2 tsp. sugar
1/2 tsp. salt
1/2 tsp. Sherry
1 tsp. oyster sauce
1 Tbsp. ginger, finely minced
9 sheets filo dough
1 beaten egg
4 cups oil

Mix all ingredients except last three. Let stand overnight in refrigerator. Cut filo sheets lengthwise into 4 equal strips. Brush one strip with a little oil, using your fingers, and lay another strip on top. Brush second strip with same amount of oil. Place 1 tablespoon filling on one end of strip, shaping filling into a cylinder. Roll filling up once, then fold left and right sides of strip 1/2-inch lengthwise to enclose the filling. Continue rolling filo all the way to the end. Seal with beaten egg. Repeat procedure with rest of filo and filling. Heat oil in wok over medium high heat. Deep fry chicken rolls until golden. Drain on paper towels. Cool slightly before serving.

CABBAGE ROLLS

1 whole Chinese cabbage
1 Tbsp. cornstarch
3/4 cup diced chicken breast
1/4 cup bamboo shoots, diced

1 Tbsp. green peas
2 tsp. light shoyu
1 tsp. sesame oil
Pinch of salt and white pepper

Remove core from cabbage and remove 8 best leaves. Parboil leaves until soft enough for easy rolling, but not too soft. Drain and pat dry with paper towels. Sprinkle evenly with cornstarch on both sides of the leaves. Combine remaining ingredients. Divide into 8 balls. Place one ball on each of the 8 leaves. Roll into little envelopes. Steam rolls on high heat for 15 minutes. Slice and serve.

SWEET-SOUR (BARBECUE) CHICKEN WINGS

40 chicken wings
1 14-oz. bottle catsup
1 8-oz. can tomato sauce
1 cup cider vinegar
Dash of Worcestershire sauce

1 tsp. dry (Colman) mustard
1 tsp. ground ginger
1 cup brown sugar
1 cup white sugar

Cut off and discard wing tips. Cut wings at joint and place in rectangular baking dish in a single layer. Mix remaining ingredients and pour over wings, turning them once to coat completely. Bake uncovered at 350° for 2 hours, turning several times, until sugar cooks down and wings are well glazed. Be certain to have enough sauce to cover the wings before baking.

NOTE: If the quantity of sauce is insufficient to cover the wings, make another half-recipe to completely cover the wings. This is a Texas-style barbecue sauce, good with short ribs, spare ribs, etc. It is a nice change from the usual teriyaki-style chicken we serve so often.

These wings will disappear in no time and I don't mean flying away!

KOREAN CHICKEN WINGS

2 lbs. chicken wings, lightly salted
2 Tbsp. flour
4 Tbsp. cornstarch
4 Tbsp. mochiko
1 Tbsp. salt
3 Tbsp. sugar
2 eggs, slightly beaten
2 Tbsp. green onion, chopped
2 tsp. chopped garlic

Lightly salt chicken wings, which may be disjointed or whole. Mix remaining ingredients; add chicken wings. The marinade will be very dry, but work in the wings a few at a time, to coat well. Marinate 4 hours or overnight and fry in just enough hot oil to cover and brown.

NOTE: When using 5 pounds of chicken wings, double the recipe. Use double plastic bags to marinate the chicken wings, securing well. Turn the bag over once during the marinating process. Very good as a picnic or potluck dish also.

PUPU KOREAN

4 pounds chicken wings
2 tsp. salt
Flour
1/2 cup shoyu
6 Tbsp. sugar
1 clove garlic, finely minced
1 stalk green onion, finely minced
1 skin of chili pepper, minced

Salt chicken and dredge in flour. Deep fry chicken wings and dip while hot in sauce made with remaining ingredients.

NOTE: Chicken tips should be cut off and wings should be disjointed to make them easier to fry and dip. Good eating and very simple.

BAKED CHICKEN WINGS

3/4 cup grated Parmesan cheese
1-1/2 tsp. parsley, chopped
3/4 cup herb-seasoned bread crumbs
1-1/2 tsp. garlic salt
16 wings, split at joints
1/2 cup melted butter

Combine cheese, parsley, bread crumbs and garlic salt.

Dip wings in butter and roll in crumb mixture.

Bake at 350° for 18 minutes or at 450° for 15 minutes. Serve warm or cold.

NOTE: This recipe is one that is both simple and fast but with good results. You will notice other recipes using grated Parmesan cheese as a coating. It has a nice flavor and texture.

Make bread crumbs by blenderizing herb-seasoned stuffing mix. Here again I had to improvise and came up with the idea of using the stuffing mix rather than mixing herbs and bread crumbs. So do the same; improvise as you go along and you will be pleased with the results. After all, a recipe is only the basis from which you can branch out as far as your imagination will take you.

CHICKEN WINGS STUFFED WITH CREAM CHEESE

2-1/2 lbs. (about 16) large chicken wings
1 Tbsp. rice wine
3 Tbsp. light shoyu

Stuffing:
6 oz. cream cheese
2 Tbsp. chopped fresh ginger
3 Tbsp. chopped scallion
2 Tbsp. fresh coriander
1 Tbsp. light shoyu
2 tsp. sesame oil

To bone chicken wings, cut to the bone above the joint joining the wing to the wing drumette. Grab the joint with a paper towel to keep your hand from slipping and twist; the bone of the drumette should come out. Push the meat up, exposing most of the bone. With your finger, make a small pocket where the bone was lodged.

Repeat the procedure for the joint between the wing and wing tip. Bone all the wings. Marinate the wings in rice wine and shoyu for 1 hour in the refrigerator.

Preheat oven to 500°. In a small bowl mix together cream cheese stuffing ingredients. Stuff about 1 teaspoon in each wing using a small spoon or your fingers.

Place the stuffed wings in a single layer in a baking pan, skin side up. Reduce oven temperature to 400° and bake wings for about 20 minutes, until golden brown.

NOTE: This is worth the bother of boning the wings.

MOCK CHICKEN LEGS

1 cup plum wine
1/4 cup shoyu
1/4 cup molasses
2 Tbsp. wine vinegar
2 scallions (green onions), minced

2 cloves garlic, minced
1 Tbsp. grated ginger
40 chicken wings (3-1/2 lbs.)
Garlic-Soy Dipping Sauce

Combine wine, shoyu, molasses, vinegar, scallions, garlic and ginger in mixing bowl and set aside.

Cut off the tips and middle* portions of the wings. Reserve for use later as stock, etc. With a sharp knife, loosen the meat around the middle joint and push the meat down gently, scraping the bone to about three-fourths of the length. Turn the meat inside out around the big joint to form a drumstick.

Marinate the chicken wings for 4 hours or overnight in the refrigerator.

Grill the wing "legs" over hot coals or in a broiler until golden brown. Serve with Garlic-Soy Dipping Sauce.

NOTE: *The middle portion of the wings may be used as with drumette section by discarding one of the two bones. Push the meat down and turn it inside out to form a mini-drumstick.

GARLIC-SOY DIPPING SAUCE:

4 Tbsp. shoyu
3 Tbsp. rice wine vinegar
2 Tbsp. vegetable oil
Pinch of sugar

1 tsp. sesame oil
1 tsp. garlic, minced
1 tsp. scallion, minced

Mix all the ingredients shortly before serving.

Serve as a dipping sauce for won ton, dumplings, meatballs, etc.

Makes 1 cup, which is enough for the preceding recipe. But this sauce is good enough to be made in a larger quantity and stored in the refrigerator to be used in everyday cooking. Just a little bit added to stir-fry dishes gives them a flavor different from most other stir-fry dishes.

CHICKEN LOAF

1 lb. chicken thighs
4 dried shiitake mushrooms, soaked in warm water until soft, then
   minced
1/2 cup scallions, minced
1/3 cup carrots, minced
2 tsp. fresh ginger juice
2 eggs
1 cup Japanese-style bread crumbs
4 tsp. miso
2 Tbsp. rice wine (sake)
Oil

Bone chicken thighs; mince the meat fine. Do not use food processor (meat may lose its texture). Add all remaining ingredients except oil and mix well until texture is paste-like.

Brush oil on a cookie sheet with edges. Spread mixture evenly about 1/3-inch thick. Preheat oven to 400°. Bake on center shelf for 15 minutes. Move the sheet to the top shelf and turn heat up to broil. Broil for 2 minutes or until the top is golden brown. Take care that the fat from the chicken does not catch on fire. (If it does, keep the oven door closed until it burns itself out. Do not open the door, as oxygen will feed the fire.)

Remove from the oven and lift the loaf onto a double thickness of paper towels to drain excess fat. Cut into 1- x 1-1/2-inch rectangles while hot. Cool and serve at room temperature.

NOTE: This freezes well after broiling. Thaw and serve.

CHICKEN WING CRISPS

3 lbs. chicken wings
1/3 cup white wine
2/3 cup corn oil
1 pkg. (.7 oz.) Good Seasons Garlic Salad Dressing Mix

Cut off wing tips and discard, cutting remaining wings in half. Place in Pyrex baking dish. Combine wine, oil and dressing mix, pour over wing sections and marinate several hours in the refrigerator.

Place in a large baking pan. Bake in 325° oven for 15-20 minutes. Turn and brush with marinade and bake 15-20 minutes longer.

Broil on both sides until crispy before serving.

NOTE: Wings can be prepared up to the point of broiling the day before and refrigerated until time to broil and serve. They can also be frozen if prepared days ahead, thawed and broiled just before serving.

This keeps well in the freezer so freeze leftovers for unexpected company. You will be known as a most gracious host or hostess.

CHICKEN YUM STICKS

5 lbs. chicken wings
3/4 cup water
1 cup soy sauce
1/4 cup pineapple juice
1/4 cup salad oil
1 tsp. garlic powder
1 tsp. grated ginger
2 Tbsp. sugar

Cut wings at first and second joints. Discard tips. Mix all ingredients above and pour over chicken in large, shallow dish and cover. Refrigerate overnight. Bake uncovered on a flat cookie sheet, 10 x 15 x 1 inch, at 350° for 45 minutes or until tender and brown, turning over several times.

SEAFOODS

PICKLED SHRIMP

12-16 peeled, uncooked shrimp, deveined
1/2 cup vinegar
1/2 cup sugar

Bring vinegar and sugar to boil. Add shrimp and cook for 4-5 minutes. Remove and serve hot or let cool in the liquid. Drain and serve cold. You may use shoyu as a dip.

NOTE: This has a very refreshing, pick-you-up taste. A different way to serve the very versatile shrimp.

FRIED SHRIMP

2-3 lbs. fresh shrimp in shell   1/3 cup wine
1 Tbsp. salt   1 tsp. sugar
1 tsp. ground ginger   2 Tbsp. cornstarch

Remove legs from shrimp. Soak in marinade made with remaining ingredients except cornstarch for 20 minutes. Dip in cornstarch and fry in about 1/2 inch of hot oil.

NOTE: Another simple fried shrimp recipe calls for marinating the shrimp overnight in oodles of garlic salt. Coat with cornstarch and fry.

BROILED SHRIMP

1-2 Tbsp. rock salt
Crushed garlic to taste
1 lb. fresh shrimp

Clean shrimp and remove legs only. Sprinkle with salt and mix in crushed garlic. Marinate for one hour and broil.

NOTE: This same mixture can be used for lean short ribs and is terrific broiled.

BROILED VINHA D'ALHOS SHRIMP

5 lbs. frozen shrimp
2 pkgs. Noh brand Vinha D'Alhos powder

Wash shrimp, remove legs if desired, and drain well. Place in a large bowl, add 2 packages Vinha D'Alhos powder and mix well. DO NOT ADD WATER. Refrigerate overnight, turning occasionally.

Broil in a single layer for 3-4 minutes on one side, turning over when shrimp turn slightly pink at the edges and continue broiling for another minute. DO NOT OVERCOOK.

NOTE: This freezes very well. All you need to do to serve is to thaw to room temperature or warm in the microwave. This is one of the easiest and best pupus. You will be surprised how fast 5 pounds of shrimp will disappear. Keep the shells on as they help retain the flavor and slow down the consumption because they have to be peeled to be eaten.

Variation: You may use the cleaned fillet of squid or fish. Be certain to score the squid to prevent it from curling when broiling.

SEAFOODS

BAKED STUFFED SHRIMP

1 cup Ritz cracker crumbs
1 cup crushed potato chips
1/4 lb. butter, melted
1 pint scallops
Seasoned salt
Milk
16-20 jumbo shrimp
Parmesan cheese

Combine first 3 ingredients. Chop scallops very fine; add them and enough milk to first ingredients to make light and fluffy stuffing. Season with onion salt, garlic salt and dash of celery salt. Split and flatten peeled shrimp. Cover each with stuffing and sprinkle with Parmesan cheese. Bake at 350° for 20 minutes or until shrimp turn white.

SHRIMP PATTIES

2 lbs. shrimp
2 bamboo shoots
2 stalks green onion
2 tsp. salt
4 eggs
Pepper to taste

Clean and chop shrimp. Add 1 tsp. salt, mix and let stand. Cut bamboo shoots and green onion fine. Beat eggs well. Add beaten eggs, finely chopped bamboo shoots and green onion, 1 tsp. salt, and pepper to shrimp and mix well. Drop by tablespoons into skillet and fry until golden brown.

NOTE: This was demonstrated by a 4-Her at contest night. Good as a side dish also.

SHRIMP-AVOCADO APPETIZER COCKTAIL

1/2 lb. shrimp, shelled, deveined, cooked and diced
1 avocado, diced
1 tsp. Pickapeppa
2 Tbsp. catsup
1 Tbsp. finely chopped ripe tomato
1 Tbsp. finely chopped green pepper
4 Tbsp. chili sauce

Combine equal parts of shrimp and avocado. Prepare sauce by mixing remaining ingredients together. Toss shrimp, avocado and sauce gently. Chill thoroughly until ready to serve. Serve with crackers or plain.

NOTE: This is my own concoction. Pickapeppa can be found in the gourmet section of most supermarkets. It is very versatile. Sprinkle generously over one 8-oz. block of softened cream cheese and serve with crackers. Very delicious. Tastes like a spicy chutney mix. Experiment with it and you will enjoy its nice flavor.

GLAZED SHRIMP HORS D'OEUVRES

1 lb. fresh shrimp, peeled, deveined, cooked and chilled
1-7/8 cups tomato juice
1/2 tsp. seasoned salt
3 oz. lemon JELL-O

Heat tomato juice with 1/2 tsp. seasoned salt. Add 3 oz. lemon JELL-O and stir until dissolved. Pour into dish to chill until thick enough to coat boiled shrimp. Repeat coating process many times until you get the thickness you desire. Chill until ready to serve. Serve a glazed shrimp on a potato chip.

NOTE: This sure beats making the glaze from scratch. If you want the glaze more tomato-y, reduce the tomato juice and replace it with the same amount of tomato paste.

SEAFOODS

SPICY SHRIMP AND BACON KABOBS

1 lb. fresh jumbo shrimp in shell
3 Tbsp. cooking oil
2 Tbsp. Pickapeppa sauce
2 Tbsp. apricot preserves
1 Tbsp. honey
1 Tbsp. maple syrup
1 tsp. crushed red pepper
1 tsp. Szechuan peppercorns,
    crushed

1/4 tsp. dried basil, crushed
1/4 tsp. dried oregano, crushed
1/4 tsp. dried rosemary, crushed
1 clove garlic, minced
3 Tbsp. lemon juice
7-8 slices bacon

Thaw shrimp; peel and devein. Stir together remaining ingredients except lemon juice and shrimp. Add shrimp, stir, cover and chill for at least 1 hour. Halve bacon slices crosswise. In 10-inch skillet, partially cook bacon. Drain well on paper towels. Drain shrimp, reserving marinade. Wrap each shrimp with a half slice of bacon; thread on 4-inch skewers. Squeeze lemon juice over kabobs and broil on a greased rack for 3-4 minutes. Turn and brush with marinade; broil 3-4 minutes more or until shrimp are done.

NOTE: Soak bamboo skewers in water at least 30 minutes before use. They will burn if you don't.

SKEWERED SHRIMP AND SCALLOPS

1/2 cup oil
1/4 cup vermouth
1/4 cup soy sauce
1/4 tsp. powdered ginger

1 clove garlic, crushed
2 lbs. large raw shrimp, shelled and
    deveined
1 pound raw scallops

Combine oil, vermouth, soy sauce, ginger and garlic to make a marinade. Marinate shrimp and scallops for 30 minutes. Thread onto bamboo skewers that have been soaked in water. Broil, turning frequently, and baste with marinade for about 5 minutes or until just cooked.

GARLIC SHRIMP

3 cloves garlic, crushed in press with skins on
2 dried red chili peppers
1 bay leaf
4 Tbsp. olive oil
1 lb. medium shrimp, unshelled, legs removed, well drained
Salt and pepper to taste

Combine garlic, whole chili peppers, bay leaf and olive oil in a sauté pan and cook over low heat for 2-3 minutes so spices will release their flavor.

Add shrimp and sauté for another 2-3 minutes, turning once, just until shrimp are pink. Do not overcook. Sprinkle with salt and pepper to taste and serve.

NOTE: This freezes very well and is good when planning a large party that requires detailed scheduling. Shrimp freezes beautifully and is enjoyed by almost everyone. Pity the poor people who are allergic to seafood. They miss out on the best of pupus.

BACON-WRAPPED SHRIMP

1 lb. medium (30-35 count) shrimp
Boiling water
1/2 lb. sliced bacon
1 clove garlic, pressed
1/2 cup tomato-based chili sauce

Cook shrimp in enough boiling water to cover until they turn pink (about 5 minutes). Drain and cool; shell and devein.

Cook bacon strips in frying pan until limp; drain and cut each slice in half crosswise. Stir together garlic and chili sauce until well blended. Dip each shrimp into sauce to coat, wrap in half strip of bacon and secure with a wooden pick. May be refrigerated until the next day at this point.

To cook, place appetizers on a broiler pan and broil 6 inches from broiler unit, turning once, until bacon is crisp (about 5 minutes. Serve hot.

NOTE: For those who love shrimp cocktails, this is a slightly different variation. Delicious!

OVEN CURRIED SHRIMP

2 lbs. shrimp
1 egg, beaten
1 Tbsp. water
1 cup dried bread crumbs, toasted
2 tsp. curry powder
1/2 tsp. salt
Dash of pepper
1/4 cup melted fat or oil

Clean and devein shrimp. Combine egg and water. Combine crumbs, curry powder, salt and pepper. Dip shrimp in egg and roll in crumbs. Place on well-greased cookie sheet. Drizzle fat over shrimp. Bake in 500° oven for 10-15 minutes, or until golden brown. Serve with Hot Marmalade Dip.

HOT MARMALADE DIP

3 cups orange marmalade
1/4 cup lemon juice
1/4 cup soy sauce
1 clove garlic, finely chopped
Dash of powdered ginger
1 tsp. cornstarch
1 Tbsp. cold water

Combine marmalade, lemon juice, soy sauce, garlic and ginger and bring to boiling point.

Dissolve cornstarch in water, add to hot sauce and cook until thickened, stirring constantly. Serve hot.

NOTE: This dip is very interesting. It can be thinned and used as a glaze for pork cutlets or other meats.

MARINATED SCALLOPS AND SHRIMP

1 lb. scallops, halved
1 lb. fresh shrimp, shelled and deveined
1/4 cup finely chopped onion
1 tsp. salt
1/4 tsp. white pepper
1 lb. fresh mushrooms, thickly sliced through stem
1 bay leaf

Lemon Dressing:
1/3 cup lemon juice
2 Tbsp. olive oil
2 tsp. salt
1/4 tsp. white pepper
2 tsp. tarragon vinegar
Chopped parsley

In medium saucepan combine scallops, shrimp, onion, bay leaf, 1 teaspoon salt, and 1/4 teaspoon pepper. Add water to cover. Bring to boil, remove from heat, cover, and let stand for 5 minutes. With slotted spoon remove scallops, shrimp and onion to shallow baking dish. Add sliced mushrooms; toss with shellfish mixture. Make lemon dressing: combine well all dressing ingredients except parsley. Pour over shellfish; toss to mix well. Refrigerate, covered, overnight. Before serving, toss well; turn into serving dish; sprinkle with parsley. Serve with picks.

MARINATED SHRIMP

Marinade:

1-1/4 cups olive oil
2/3 cup tarragon vinegar
1/2 tsp. salt
1/4 tsp. black pepper
1/4 tsp. paprika
1 large onion, coarsely chopped

1 clove garlic, mashed
3 Tbsp. Dijon mustard
1 Tbsp. German-style mustard
2 Tbsp. prepared horseradish
1 Tbsp. powdered thyme

1-2 lbs. jumbo shrimp

Place all ingredients except the shrimp in a blender and blend until onion is finely minced. Cook the shrimp in boiling salted water about 3 minutes; then rinse under cold running water to stop the cooking process. Remove shells and chill shrimp in the marinade until icy cold. Drain off marinade and serve it separately as a dip for the shrimp.

SHRIMP TEMPURA

1 lb. large shrimp

Batter:

1 cup flour
1 cup cornstarch
1-2/3 cups cold water

1 egg
Salt to taste
1/4 tsp. baking powder

Butterfly shrimp, leaving tails on. Mix ingredients for batter. Let stand 10 minutes. Dip shrimp in cornstarch, then into batter, and fry in 1/2 inch hot oil. Use fingers to drop more batter on top of shrimp in oil. Turn after a minute. Serve with dipping sauce. Shrimp should not be overcooked. When it turns pink it is done.

DIPPING SAUCE

1/2 cup chicken broth
2 Tbsp. shoyu
2 Tbsp. mirin (sweet cooking sauce)

Heat ingredients only until warm and use for shrimp tempura dip.

SHRIMP JAMBALAYA

1 cup sliced celery
2 cups diced green pepper
2 medium onions, thinly sliced
4 Tbsp. butter, divided in half
2 cloves garlic, minced
1 lb. cooked ham, 3/4 in. thick, cubed
2 lbs. peeled, deveined shrimp, coarsely
　chopped

1-1/2 tsp. salt
1/4 tsp. hot pepper sauce
1/2 tsp. chili powder
1 tsp. sugar
2 cans (1 lb. each)
　whole tomatoes
3 cups hot cooked rice

Cook celery, green pepper and onion in half the butter until tender but not brown. Add garlic and ham and cook 5 minutes longer. Add remaining butter, shrimp, salt, hot pepper sauce, chili powder and sugar. Cook, tossing often with fork until shrimp are pink. Add tomatoes, heat, and stir in rice. Serve warm on toast squares.

NOTE: This is a main-dish recipe, but is very good and something unusual to serve as a pupu, especially if you use toast squares.

SHOYU SHRIMP

1 lb. shrimp
1 stalk green onion, chopped
1 piece ginger
1 clove garlic, crushed
3/4 cup stock or water

Marinade:
1/2 tsp. sugar
1 Tbsp. liquor
1/2 tsp. thick shoyu
1/4 tsp. sesame oil
2 Tbsp. shoyu

Wash shrimp and remove legs. Soak in marinade for 20 minutes. To hot pan add oil, ginger, garlic and shrimp. Fry 1-2 minutes. Add remaining sauce and stock and bring to boil. Thicken with cornstarch and add chopped green onions before taking it off the stove.

NOTE: This is good also on your dinner menu or as a side dish. Good with hot rice.

ORIENTAL SHRIMP TOAST

3 strips raw bacon
1 lb. raw shrimp, peeled and deveined
1/2 cup water chestnuts, finely chopped
1/4 cup green onion, chopped
2 Tbsp. parsley, chopped
1 tsp. white wine
12 slices white bread, crust removed

With cleaver or sharp knife, mince shrimp and bacon until it forms a paste. Stir in water chestnuts, green onions, parsley and white wine. Spread mixture onto bread. Cover with plastic wrap and refrigerate until ready to deep fry.

Heat oil to 350°. Fry bread with shrimp-mixture-side down until edges begin to brown. Turn over and cook until lightly browned on all sides. Drain on paper towels, cut each square into 4 triangles with sharp knife and serve hot.

NOTE: Keep in 250° oven until serving time. It can also be frozen and reheated in 450° oven for about 5-7 minutes, but because of our humidity, toast will turn soggy after being out for a while. That's the price of paradise!

CHINESE BARBECUED SHRIMP

2 lbs. raw shrimp, shelled and deveined
3/4 tsp. salt
Dash of pepper
1 Tbsp. honey
2 Tbsp. shoyu
1 Tbsp. dry Sherry
3 Tbsp. vegetable oil

Place shrimp in a flat baking dish. Combine remaining ingredients and marinate shrimp for 15 minutes. Bake at 375° for 10 minutes.

NOTE: This can be prepared and frozen. Thaw, heat and serve.

TOFU AND SHRIMP WITH HOISIN SAUCE

3 Tbsp. hoisin sauce
2 Tbsp. rice vinegar
2 Tbsp. water
2 tsp. sugar
1/2 tsp. ground ginger
1/2 tsp. cornstarch
1/8 tsp. crushed red pepper
2 Tbsp. vegetable oil
14 oz. tofu, drained, cut in 1-in. cubes
1/2 medium shrimp, shelled and deveined
1 clove garlic, minced or pressed
6 green onions, cut in 1-in. lengths

Combine hoisin sauce, vinegar, water, sugar, ginger and cornstarch and set aside. Heat 1 tablespoon oil in large skillet over medium-high heat; add tofu cubes and stir-fry about 2 minutes or until lightly browned on all sides. Remove from skillet and set aside.

Add 1 tablespoon oil to skillet; stir-fry garlic and shrimp for 2 minutes over medium-high heat, stirring constantly. Stir in green onion and hoisin sauce mixture and red pepper and cook, stirring until thickened and shrimp turns slightly pink, about 3 minutes. Add tofu and combine well, stirring carefully so as not to break up tofu cubes.

NOTE: If you do not like spicy-hot food, decrease the amount of crushed red pepper.

TEA-SMOKED SHRIMP

Grated rind and juice of 2 oranges
1 tsp. salt
2 Tbsp. rice wine vinegar
30 large shrimp, unpeeled
1/2 cup loose tea, preferably oolong or Earl Grey
1/2 cup sugar
1 tsp. cayenne pepper

Combine the orange rind and juice, salt and vinegar in a mixing bowl. Add the shrimp and marinate them overnight.

To smoke the shrimp, line a heavy dutch oven with aluminum foil. Sprinkle the tea, sugar and cayenne pepper on the foil and set a rack over it. Cover the pot tightly and turn the flame to high. The sugar will melt, and the pot will start smoking. (Keep a kitchen exhaust fan going at all times to clear the smoke.) Turn off the flame, lay the shrimp on the rack, recover, and turn the flame to high. Smoke the shrimp for 5 or 6 minutes. Do not overcook, or the shrimp will become tough.

Cool the shrimp and keep refrigerated until ready to serve. They will keep in the refrigerator for about a week.

NOTE: The shrimp will turn delightfully brown and look very delicious.

SPICY STIR-FRIED SHRIMP

1 lb. medium shrimp in shells
2 Tbsp. peanut oil
2 Tbsp. chopped scallions with tops
1 Tbsp. Chinese salted black beans, rinsed, drained
2 tsp. minced fresh ginger
2 cloves garlic, minced
1 tsp. finely chopped fresh hot green chili pepper
1 Tbsp. sesame oil
1 Tbsp. dark soy sauce
1 tsp. Chinese chili paste
1 tsp. oyster sauce

Split shrimp through shells down center of back to remove dark veins. Do not remove shrimp from shells or remove the legs. Wash and drain.

Heat large heavy skillet over high heat until hot enough to evaporate a bead of water on contact. Add peanut oil. Swirl to coat pan evenly.

When oil is fragrant, add scallions, black beans, ginger, garlic and chili pepper; stir-fry until garlic is fragrant, about 1 minute. Add shrimp, sesame oil, soy sauce, chili paste and oyster sauce. Cook, stirring constantly, until shrimp shells turn pink and shrimp feel firm when pressed between your fingers, about 4-5 minutes.

Serve shrimp in shells at room temperature or cold.

SZECHUAN SHRIMP

2 Tbsp. peanut oil
1 lb. extra-large shrimp, shelled, deveined
1/4 cup minced green onion
2 Tbsp. minced ginger
3 cloves garlic, minced
2 Tbsp. dry Sherry
2 Tbsp. soy sauce
2 tsp. sugar
1/2 tsp. salt
3 Tbsp. catsup
2 Tbsp. chili sauce
1 tsp. red pepper flakes

Heat oil in wok or large heavy skillet. Add shrimp, green onion, ginger and garlic. Stir-fry until shrimp are pink. Add Sherry, soy sauce, sugar and salt. Stir well and blend in catsup, chili sauce and red pepper flakes.

TORRID SHRIMP

1 lb. shrimp
3 cloves garlic, crushed
1/2 cup lemon juice
1 tsp. salt
3 hot red peppers

Cook shrimp in boiling water for 5 minutes. Drain and plunge into ice water. Shell and devein shrimp. Put in deep bowl. In another bowl blend remaining ingredients. Pour over shrimp. Let stand 4-5 hours. Drain shrimp. Serve on cocktail picks.

SHRIMP IN BEER I

5 lbs. shrimp in shell
2 cans beer
1 cup water
1/2 box bay leaves
1/2 box celery seed
Salt

Wash shrimp in cold water. Mix beer and water in deep kettle in which colander will fit. Layer shrimp, bay leaves, celery seed and 1/2 handful of salt per layer, in about 3 layers. Cover tightly and cook at slow boil for 20-30 minutes. To serve, dip in melted butter.

NOTE: Very good for large gatherings.

SHRIMP IN BEER II

1 quart beer
4 Tbsp. lemon juice
2 tsp. salt
1 tsp. whole peppercorns
1 tsp. dried tarragon
2 lbs. raw shrimp in shell

Combine beer with seasonings in saucepan. Bring to a boil and simmer 10 minutes. Add shrimp and bring back to a boil. Lower heat and simmer 2-5 more minutes until shrimp turns pink. Drain, cool and shell shrimp. Chill and serve cold.

NOTE: Again, do not overcook shrimp. It will toughen and shrink.

SCAMPI I

2 lbs. large prawns, shelled except for tail
1 oz. butter
1 oz. olive oil
1/4 tsp. freshly ground black pepper
1/4 tsp. salt
2 oz. dry vermouth
Juice of 2 lemons
1 clove garlic, crushed

Heat olive oil in large skillet. When oil is simmering add prawns and allow to cook until golden brown. Reduce heat and add butter, garlic, salt and pepper. When well blended, increase fire to very hot. Add lemon juice and dry vermouth and cook 1 minute longer, constantly stirring or shaking.

SCAMPI II

1/2 lb. shrimp
1 stick butter
1 clove garlic
1/4 cup chopped green onion
Salt to taste

Wash shrimp and remove legs only. Melt butter on low heat to prevent burning. Add drained shrimp and turn heat up slightly. Add grated garlic and salt to taste when shrimp starts to turn pink. Cook only until shrimp has turned completely pink. Just before removing from heat, add chopped green onions.

NOTE: This is my own concoction. If prepared in large quantities, keep in chafing dish or on warming tray since the butter will tend to get greasy if left out for any length of time. The shell on the shrimp helps retain the flavor. Shrimp should not be overcooked, since it will get touch and shrink.

SAUTÉED PRAWNS

16-20 prawns, peeled and deveined
2 Tbsp. shoyu
1 Tbsp. sugar
2 Tbsp. water
1 clove garlic, chopped
2 Tbsp. oil for frying

Marinate prawns for 1 hour or more in shoyu, sugar, water and garlic. Drain and quickly fry in hot oil, turning continually. Serve hot.

FISHERMAN'S PRAWNS

2-1/2 lbs. jumbo prawns
1/4 cup olive oil
1 tsp. salt
1 tsp. leaf oregano
1 clove garlic, chopped
1/3 cup prepared horseradish
3/4 cup dry white wine
3 oz. lemon juice
1/2 cup orange marmalade

Shell, clean and devein prawns. Rinse well; drain on paper towels. Combine remaining ingredients. Place prawns in 13- x 9-inch Pyrex dish. Cover with marinade. Refrigerate 2 or more hours. Preheat large shallow casserole containing enough marinade to cover bottom of dish. Add prawns. Broil for 3-4 minutes or until prawns are tender, turning occasionally. Do not overcook.

SEAFOOD BAKE

1 can cream of mushroom soup
1/3 cup mayonnaise
1/3 cup milk
6 oz. canned shrimp, drained
7 oz. crabmeat, drained
5 oz. water chestnuts
1 cup diced celery
2 tsp. grated onion
2 cups cooked rice
1-1/2 cups fresh bread crumbs
3 Tbsp. melted butter

Combine all ingredients except crumbs and melted butter in a 2-quart casserole. Combine crumbs and melted butter and sprinkle on top. Bake at 350° for one hour.

NOTE: Serve in individual custard dishes with crackers for dipping.

CRAB DELIGHT

1 envelope unflavored gelatin
3 Tbsp. cold water
1 can cream of mushroom soup
6 oz. cream cheese, softened
2/3 cup mayonnaise
1 cup finely chopped celery
1/2 lb. crabmeat, fresh frozen
1 small onion, grated
Parsley for garnish

Soften gelatin in cold water. Warm soup to simmering; add softened gelatin and cream cheese. Stir over medium heat until dissolved, about 3 minutes. Remove from heat and add mayonnaise, celery, crabmeat and grated onion. Rinse 4-cup mold in cold water. Pour mixture into mold and refrigerate overnight. Unmold on a cold serving platter and garnish with parsley. Serve with crackers.

CRABMEAT TOAST

1/2 lb. meat of king crab legs
1 tsp. dry Sherry
1 tsp. salt
1/4 tsp. white pepper
1 Tbsp. chopped fresh dill or 1 tsp. dried dill
1 Tbsp. butter
2 Tbsp. flour
1 egg yolk
1 cup light cream
1 loaf sandwich bread, crust trimmed

Combine crabmeat, Sherry, salt, pepper and dill in a large mixing bowl and set aside.

Melt butter in a saucepan, remove from heat and stir in flour. In a small bowl beat the egg yolk with cream, then briskly stir into flour/butter roux with wire whisk. Return pan to stove and cook slowly, whisking constantly for 1-2 minutes or until mixture thickens. Do not let it boil. Pour sauce over crabmeat and stir until well combined.

Toast bread on one side only. Spread untoasted side generously with crabmeat mixture, mounding it slightly. May be prepared in advance up to this point and refrigerated. Before serving, place under hot broiler for a minute or so until hot and lightly browned. Cut into fourths and serve.

CURRIED CRAB TRIANGLES

2 Tbsp. onion, chopped
2 Tbsp. butter
1/4 cup mushrooms, chopped
1/4 tsp. curry powder
1/2 cup frozen crab leg meat
1/2 cup mayonnaise
1/4 cup grated Parmesan cheese
6 slices bread, crust removed and toasted on one side

Sauté onion and mushrooms in butter. Add curry powder and shredded crabmeat. Remove from heat.

Stir in mayonnaise and spread on untoasted side of bread. Sprinkle with cheese and broil until cheese is bubbly.

Cut each square into 4 triangles and serve.

NOTE: This can be frozen before broiling. Lay toast slices in a single layer on a baking sheet and freeze. When frozen, pack in Ziplock freezer bag until ready to use.

To serve, partially thaw and broil until done. Cut in triangles and serve.

CRABMEAT PUFF SHELLS

Puff Pastry:
1/4 cup shortening
1/2 cup boiling water
1/2 cup flour
1/4 tsp. salt
2 eggs

On high heat bring water to a boil, add shortening and cook until melted. Add flour and salt. Continue cooking on high heat, stirring constantly until dough forms a ball and leaves the sides of the pan. Cool 3-4 minutes and beat in eggs, one at a time, beating well after each addition. Drop by 1/2 teaspoonfuls on greased baking sheet and bake at 400° for 10 minutes. Yields 40-50 puffs.

Filling:
1 cup crabmeat
1/4 cup lime juice
3 oz. cream cheese
1/4 cup heavy cream
2 Tbsp. mayonnaise
Pinch of salt
1 Tbsp. minced onion
1 clove garlic, minced
1 tsp. finely chopped chives
1/4 tsp. Tabasco
1 tsp. Worcestershire sauce

Marinate crabmeat in lime juice for 30 minutes. Whip cream cheese and cream, add remaining ingredients and fold in crabmeat. Fill puffs. Bake at 375° for 10 minutes. Serve warm.

CRABMEAT BALLS

1 cup crabmeat from king crab legs
3 Tbsp. butter
1/4 cup bread crumbs
1 Tbsp. minced onion
3 Tbsp. finely chopped celery
1/4 tsp. prepared mustard
1 large egg, beaten
1/8 tsp. paprika
1 tsp. lemon juice
Salt and pepper
Dash of Worcestershire sauce

Melt butter in skillet. Add onion and simmer 3 minutes. Add bread crumbs and stir over heat another 2 minutes. Add other ingredients and mix well.

Form into balls measuring approximately 3/4 to 1 inch. Dust your hands with flour or bread crumbs when forming balls. (The balls may be frozen on a cookie sheet, bagged and stored until ready for use.)

Broil 3-5 minutes or until slightly browned.

NOTE: If balls are frozen, thaw on the broiler pan and broil until slightly browned.

CRABMEAT ROLLS

8 slices fresh white bread
8 slices processed cheese
6 oz. crabmeat, fresh frozen
2 Tbsp. mayonnaise
1 Tbsp. green pepper, finely chopped
1/4 tsp. salt
2 Tbsp. melted butter

Trim edges of bread and cut each slice into two triangles. Place 1/2 slice of cheese on each triangle. Combine all other ingredients except melted butter and spoon mixture onto rolls by tablespoonfuls. Roll up and place seam end down on cookie sheet and refrigerate until firm. Brush with melted butter and bake at 375° for 15-20 minutes or until rolls are brown and toasted.

NOTE: The original recipe used ready-mix rolls, but they left an unpleasant aftertaste, so I substituted white bread. If the bread is not fresh enough, it will crack when you try to roll it, Try rolling it flat with a rolling pin and continue from there.

CRAB SWISS CRISPS

1 Dungeness crab, cooked
1-1/2 Tbsp. sliced green onion
1-1/4 cups shredded Swiss cheese
1/2 cup mayonnaise
1 tsp. lemon juice
1/4 tsp. curry powder
Wheat Thins

Mix all ingredients except Wheat Thins. Chill. Serve with Wheat Thins.

BROILED CRAB TIDBITS

1/4 lb. butter
1 5-oz. jar Old English cheese
1-1/2 tsp. mayonnaise
1 tsp. garlic salt
1 tsp. seasoned salt
8 oz. crabmeat, fresh frozen
6 English muffins

Soften butter and cheese and blend. Stir in mayonnaise, seasonings and flaked crabmeat. Split muffins in half and spread with mixture. Freeze 2 hours or longer and cut into 4 to 6 wedges. They can be broiled for immediate use or returned to the freezer for use whenever needed. Broil until cheese is nice and bubbly.

NOTE: Do not let this thaw before broiling. The cheese will melt away if you do. Always good to keep on hand to serve at a moment's notice.

CRAB CANAPÉS

1 cup crabmeat, fresh frozen
1 Tbsp. lemon juice
1/2 tsp. salt
1/2 tsp. celery salt
1/4 tsp. Worcestershire sauce
1 Tbsp. mayonnaise

Shred crabmeat and add remaining ingredients. Spread on rounds of buttered bread and toast in oven until lightly browned and bubbly.

CRAB WON TON POUCHES

1/2 lb. fresh crabmeat, drained
8 oz. cream cheese, softened
2 Tbsp. mayonnaise
1/2 tsp. A-1 sauce
2 Tbsp. chopped water chestnuts
1 Tbsp. grated onion
1/4 tsp. garlic powder
24 won ton wrappers
1 egg yolk, well beaten
Oil for deep frying

Chop drained crabmeat fine. Mix softened cream cheese with mayonnaise and A-1 sauce. Add water chestnuts, grated onion, garlic powder and crabmeat and mix well. Drop by teaspoonfuls in center of won ton wrappers. Spread beaten egg yolk on edges of each wrapper and gather edges up to form a pouch. You can fry in hot oil immediately, if you are ready to serve, or refrigerate the pouches at this point and fry just before serving.

NOTE: The oil should not be too hot. The won ton will get too dark and brittle and all the cheese will melt to nothing. It can be frozen. Thaw until filling is slightly soft before you begin frying if pouches have been frozen. Can be served plain or with any dipping sauce of your choice.

BROILED CRAB AND AVOCADO

3 Tbsp. flour
3 Tbsp. butter
1 cup milk
1/2 tsp. salt
1/8 tsp. white pepper
1/4 cup grated Swiss cheese
1/4 cup grated Parmesan cheese
1-1/2 cups cooked shrimp
1/2 cup meat of king crab legs
4 medium avocados
Lemon juice
Paprika

In medium saucepan, over moderate, heat, melt butter. Add flour and stir with whisk until well blended. Cook for 1 minute. Gradually add milk, whisking constantly until smooth and thick. Add seasonings and cheese and whisk until melted. Add seafood.

Cut avocados in half, leaving skin intact, but removing the pit. Rub inside with lemon juice. Heap seafood mixture onto avocado shells; place on a baking sheet. Dust with paprika. Broil until mixture bubbles. Cut halves into quarters or chunks, depending on the consistency of the filling.

NOTE: Island people prefer avocado served cut up rather than halved. You can also remove the skin and cut them in chunks, mix with the crab mixture and bake in a casserole dish at 350° until it bubbles. Serve warm.

BAKED CRAB ALASKA

4 Tbsp. butter
1/3 cup all-purpose flour
1/3 cup mayonnaise
1 4-oz. can sliced mushrooms or 1 cup sliced fresh mushrooms
 sautéed in butter
Mushroom juices and light cream to make 2 cups
1/4 cup dry Sherry
6 eggs, separated
1/2 tsp. Worcestershire sauce
3/4 tsp. salt
1/4 tsp. white pepper
1/8 tsp. cayenne pepper
2 cups flaked crabmeat, fresh frozen
12 thin slices white bread, trimmed and buttered on one side
1/2 tsp. salt
1/2 tsp. cream of tartar
1 cup freshly grated Parmesan cheese

Melt butter in large, heavy saucepan until foamy. Add flour, blend and cook for 3 minutes. Stir in mayonnaise. Drain mushrooms, reserving juice, and set aside. Blend mushroom juice-cream mixture into flour mixture. Cook and stir until well blended and thickened. Remove from heat. Beat egg yolks and Sherry until creamy and gradually stir in half the cream sauce. Add this mixture to remaining cream sauce, return to heat and stir without allowing to boil for 3 minutes. Add Worcestershire sauce, salt, pepper, cayenne, mushrooms and crab. Cut buttered bread in fourths. Place the 48 pieces of bread 2 inches apart on large cookie sheets and spread with the crab mixture on the buttered side. Chill thoroughly. Preheat oven to 375°. Beat egg whites and 1/2 tsp. salt until foamy. Add cream of tartar and beat until stiff but not dry. Spread on top and sides of each openface sandwich, sealing completely. Sprinkle with Parmesan cheese and bake for 15-20 minutes until golden brown.

NOTE: This recipe takes time and effort to prepare, but the results are well worth the effort. Believe me.

IMITATION CRAB NAMASU

1 medium round onion
1 stalk celery, minced
1 stalk green onion, minced
1 pkg. imitation crab
Black pepper to taste

Cut onion in half and slice very thin. Shred crab and mix all ingredients together and season with black pepper.

Optional: You may add a little shoyu and sesame oil if you want more taste.

NOTE: This should be prepared at least a half day before serving. The flavors blend better if you let it sit a while.

BAKED IMITATION CRAB

1 lb. imitation crab
1/2 cup shredded Parmesan cheese
1 cup mayonnaise

Place imitation crab in 8-in. baking pan. Cover with mayonnaise and sprinkle with cheese. Bake at 350° for 10-15 minutes or until cheese is lightly browned.

NOTE: This can be made into a very nice main dish by simply putting cooked broccoli or asparagus under the crab before baking.

For those who must watch their cholesterol, Saffola mayonnaise can be used sparingly in place of regular mayonnaise.

SCALLOPS NEWBURG

1 lb. scallops	2 egg yolks
3 Tbsp. butter	2 Tbsp. Sherry
1 tsp. lemon juice	1/2 lb. mushrooms
1 tsp. flour	Salt
1/2 cup cream	Cayenne pepper

Slice mushrooms. Clean scallops and cut in half. Cook 3 minutes with 2 tablespoons butter. Add lemon juice. Cook 1 minute and set aside. Blend 1 tablespoon butter, 1 teaspoon flour and 1/2 cup cream in saucepan over low heat. Stir constantly over low to medium heat and bring to boiling point. Add 2 egg yolks, slightly beaten, and 2 tablespoons Sherry. Add the scallops and mushrooms. Reduce heat and stir well. If mixture curdles from overcooking, add a little milk and stir until smooth again. Season to taste with salt and cayenne.

SCALLOP KEBABS

12 strips bacon	1-1/2 Tbsp. sugar
16 sea scallops, halved	1 Tbsp. dry Sherry
16 small water chestnuts, halved	1 clove garlic, minced
1/3 cup shoyu	1 tsp. minced ginger
2 Tbsp. rice vinegar	32 5- to 6-inch bamboo skewers

Partially cook bacon strips and cut into pieces the same size as scallops. Alternate bacon between scallops and water chestnuts on skewers. Arrange in shallow dish. Combine remaining ingredients in blender and mix well. Pour over kebabs. Cover and marinate in refrigerator for 2-3 hours, turning frequently. Grill or broil until scallops are barely firm—about 6 minutes per side.

NOTE: When skewering water chestnuts, grasp the chestnut firmly and turn the skewer slowly as you push it through. This will prevent the water chestnut from splitting in half.

MARINATED BROILED SCALLOPS

2 lbs. medium scallops
1/2 cup melted butter
1 tsp. garlic salt
3 Tbsp. lemon juice
2 tsp. shoyu
1/4 cup sherry
Paprika
Bread crumbs

Mix together butter, garlic salt, lemon juice and shoyu. Pour over scallops and marinate for one hour. Drain, reserving liquid. Broil scallops until lightly browned. Add sherry to marinade and spoon over scallops. Sprinkle with bread crumbs and paprika and continue broiling another 1-2 minutes longer.

OYSTERS PARMESAN

1/4 cup olive oil
1/4 cup light vegetable oil
2-3 cloves garlic, crushed
1 cup finely grated Parmesan cheese
1 cup finely crushed Ritz crackers
1 pint raw oysters, shucked

Combine oils and garlic in a small bowl. Drain oysters and pat dry with paper towels. Dip oysters into Parmesan cheese, then the oil mixture and finally into cracker crumbs.

Place in a 9-inch square baking dish and bake at 375° for 15 minutes.

BROILED OYSTERS

24 small oysters
1 Tbsp. flour
2 Tbsp. onion, finely minced
1/4 cup shoyu
1-1/2 Tbsp. rice wine
Oil

Place shucked oysters in a bowl, add flour, and mix thoroughly to clean. Rinse under cold water and drain.

Mince onion and combine with shoyu and rice wine in a bowl. Add the oysters and coat thoroughly. Set aside to marinate for 15 minutes.

Heat oven broiler. Oil shallow broiling pan lightly and lay oysters out in a single layer. Broil about 4 minutes, turn oysters and broil another 3-4 minutes.

Serve warm or at room temperature.

NOTE: The oysters will have a teriyaki flavor. In the process of broiling, the oysters will shrink, so don't be surprised that 24 oysters will yield only a handful or several mouthfuls.

If you prefer, this can be coated with flour or bread crumbs and deep fried.

OYSTERS ROCKEFELLER

24 oysters in shells
2 Tbsp. onion, chopped
2 Tbsp. butter, melted
2 Tbsp. parsley, chopped
1/8 tsp. paprika
Salt
Pepper
1 cup cooked spinach, chopped fine
1/4 cup fine dry bread crumbs
1/2 cup butter or margarine
Rock salt

If you use shucked oysters, prepare them in small baking shells. Open the oysters with an oyster knife. Remove the oysters from their shells and drain very well. Wash the shells. Place each oyster in the deep half of the shell.

Combine parsley, onion and the melted butter. Spread this over each oyster. Sprinkle each one with a little salt, pepper and paprika. Top each with 2 teaspoons spinach, then 1/2 teaspoon bread crumbs. Dot each one with about 1 teaspoon of butter. Arrange oyster shells on a bed of rock salt in a shallow pan. The salt will hold the shells upright. Bake at 450° until browned, about 8 to 10 minutes.

CLAM TOAST

1 10-oz. can clams
2 Tbsp. olive oil
1 medium onion, finely chopped
4 Tbsp. parsley, minced
2 cloves garlic, minced
1/2 dried red chili pepper or 1/4 tsp. crushed red pepper
4 tsp. flour
4 slices bread, crust removed, cut in 2 triangles, slightly toasted

Strain liquid from can of clams, reserve 1/3 cup—if less, add bottled clam juice or water. Chop the clams.

Heat oil in skillet and sauté onions slowly until wilted. Cover and continue cooking another 20 minutes until onion is tender. Uncover, turn up heat slightly, and add garlic, parsley and chili pepper.

Cook another 2-3 minutes; then stir in flour. Add reserved clam juice and clams and cook over medium-high heat until mixture is thick enough to spread.

Spread on toasted triangles and serve.

NOTE: This can be frozen in a single layer on a cookie sheet and bagged when frozen. To serve, thaw and warm in microwave.

BROILED CLAMS

1 lb. clams (fresh frozen)
1/4 cup mirin or sake
1/4 cup shoyu
1 Tbsp. miso
2 Tbsp. sugar

Mix mirin or sake, shoyu, miso, and sugar and bring to a boil. String 3-4 clams on bamboo skewers, dip in sauce and broil over charcoal fire.

NOTE: Very easy and very delicious.

CLAMS CASINO

2 dozen small clams
Salt to taste
Pepper to taste
Oregano to taste
2-3 cloves garlic, minced
1/4 cup butter, cut in 24 pats
1 cup Sauterne
4-6 strips bacon

Open clamshells and remove clams; reserve juice and half of the shells. Place shells on baking sheet. On each, place a clam, a small amount of juice, salt, pepper, oregano, a dab of garlic, butter, a cupful of wine and a square of bacon. Broil until bacon is crisp.

NOTE: Elegant and easy to prepare.

FRIED ABALONE

1 stick butter
1 can abalone
1-2 cloves garlic, minced

Slice abalone and fry in butter. Add minced garlic to taste. Serve warm.

NOTE: In these days when abalone is so scarce, substitute boned chicken breast that has been marinated in 1/2 cup clam juice, 1/2 cup white wine and 1/2 teaspoon garlic salt overnight.

ABALONE SALMON MIX

1 can abalone
3- to 4-inch pieces of salmon, presoaked
1 round onion, thinly sliced
Lemon juice to taste
1 large tomato, thickly sliced
1/4 cup shoyu
1 chili pepper, sliced and seeded

Slice abalone; strip salmon to bite size. Mix with round onion slices and tomatoes and season with lemon juice, chili pepper and shoyu. Chill and serve.

NOTE: Vary the shoyu and lemon according to taste.

SHOYU ABALONE

1 can abalone and juice
5 Tbsp. shoyu

1 Tbsp. brown sugar
4 Tbsp. rice vinegar

Add shoyu, sugar and vinegar to the juice. Pour over sliced abalone and refrigerate overnight before serving.

ABALONE SASHIMI

Fresh frozen abalone
Juice of one lemon
Shoyu
Chili pepper

Clean fresh frozen abalone and slice very thin. Dip in lemon, shoyu and chili pepper mixture.

DRIED ABALONE

1 cup Hawaiian (rock) salt
Fresh frozen abalone, cleaned
1/3 to 1/2 gallon water

Soak abalone overnight in saltwater brine. Bake at 200° for 4-5 hours and dry in hot sun several days until thoroughly dried. Keep flies away from it while it is drying.

CANNED ABALONE

Fresh frozen abalone
Sherry wine to cover
Garlic salt to taste

Clean fresh abalone, soak with enough wine to cover and marinate overnight in refrigerator. Place in pot with wine and simmer for 2 hours, adding garlic salt to taste. Cool, cut, serve and watch it disappear. Soft and delicious.

NOTE: If the abalone is not soft in 2 hours, cook longer until it is soft to the touch. Cooking time depends on how fresh the abalone is.

SHOYU-LEMON SQUID

3 lbs. calamari (squid)
1 cup shoyu
Juice of 2 lemons
1/4 cup sesame oil
1 Tbsp. sesame seeds, toasted
1 small onion, thinly sliced
Tabasco, 9 squirts, or 2 chili peppers, sliced

The day before, clean squid by inserting knife into the body cavity and slitting it open. Clean the inside, removing the center membrane and everything else in it. Discard what you remove except the legs, cutting just below the eyes. Separate legs by cutting into 3-4 separate groups. Bring medium pot of water to a rolling boil. Place squid into the pot, stirring to cook all the pieces. As soon as the squid starts to curl (it will take only a few seconds), drain into a colander and run under the faucet to stop the cooking process. Drain well. Cut the body pieces in half lengthwise and slice across the body into 1/4- to 1/8-inch strips.

Prepare marinade with remaining ingredients and add the squid. Refrigerate overnight.

NOTE: It sounds complicated and bothersome, but once you have done it, you will find it is fairly easy. The resulting good taste and the compliments you will receive will make it worth your while to make it again and again. The shoyu-lemon combination gives it a very good flavor. Makes about 1-1/2 quarts.

KOREAN TAKO

1 lb. fresh frozen tako (octopus)
2 Tbsp. shoyu
1 Tbsp. sugar
2 Tbsp. sesame oil

1 tsp. sesame seeds
6 green onions, sliced
1 chili pepper, crushed

Slice tako into bite-sized pieces and marinate in remaining ingredients. Chill until time to serve.

NOTE: This is very simple: requires no cooking and is very tasty. Add more shoyu if you do not like it as sweet.

HOT RAW SQUID

Clean squid, removing insides and cutting it open. Slice into strips. Mix with Hawaiian (rock) salt and cayenne pepper to taste. Refrigerate for 2-4 hours. Squeeze fresh lemon juice over squid before eating.

NOTE: Those who like raw seafood will enjoy this. The lemon juice gives it a nice taste. If you like chili pepper, you can substitute that for the cayenne.

FRIED SQUID

Fresh frozen squid, large size
Flour

Salt
Oil

Clean squid and cut body open to form a triangle. Cut squid across the body into about 1-inch strips. Flour strips generously and drop a few at a time into deep hot oil. Fry until the flour is nicely browned and crisp. Drain and add salt before serving.

NOTE: Do not add salt before frying. It will toughen the squid.

CHARCOAL BROILED VINHA D'ALHOS SQUID

3 lbs. calamari (squid)
1 pkg. Vinha D'Alhos mix powder

Clean squid, removing insides and cutting it open. Marinate with the powder and let stand for 2 hours. Broil over charcoal quickly, just until done. Do not overcook.

SALMON CEVICHE

2 lbs. salmon fillets, boned and cut into 1/2-in. pieces
1-1/2 cups fresh lemon juice
2 medium tomatoes, seeded and diced
1 medium red onion, diced
1/2 cup olive oil
1/3 cup fresh lime juice
2 whole canned green chiles, rinsed and diced
1 Tbsp. chopped cilantro (Chinese parsley)
2 garlic cloves, minced
1/2 tsp. cumin
Dash hot pepper sauce

Combine salmon and lemon juice in a bowl. Cover and refrigerate overnight, stirring occasionally. Drain salmon well and mix with remaining ingredients. Chill before serving.

NOTE: I had always wanted to try this and finally did. It has a very appealing look with the red tomatoes and red onion. It has a very delicate flavor. Those who like lemon may wish to use more lemon juice.

CHERRY TOMATOES WITH LOMI SALMON

1 pkg. salmon (about 1/2 lb.)
3 medium tomatoes, chopped
1 medium round onion, chopped
1 medium bunch green onion, chopped
1 1-lb. 14-oz. can cooked tomatoes
Cherry tomatoes

Soak salmon in water for half an hour. Strip skin, remove the bones, slice the meat into strips and chop fine. Cut tomatoes into slices and chop coarsely. Chop round onion. Slice green onions into 1/8-inch slices, add 2 tablespoons rock salt and mix well into the green onion. Rinse under running water and repeat. This will remove any of the slimy liquid from the green onion. Squeeze liquid out of the green onion. Mix salmon and fresh tomatoes well, add canned tomatoes with liquid and mash well with your hands. Add round onion and green onion. Add seeds and insides of the cherry tomatoes to this salmon mixture by cutting off the top of each cherry tomato and scooping the insides out. Add cold water to salmon mixture if there is insufficient liquid. Stuff the cherry tomatoes, chill and serve.

NOTE: The canned tomato gives this lomi salmon a slightly tart flavor that everyone will marvel about.

PORTUGUESE-STYLE AKU

1/2 cup vinegar
1/2 cup water
1 clove garlic, crushed
2 lbs. aku cut 5/8 in. thick
1-1/2 tsp. salt
1/4 tsp. pepper
1/2 cup flour
1/4 cup salad oil

Mix vinegar, water, and garlic. Pour over fish slices and marinate for one hour. Remove fish from marinade and pat dry. Coat with flour. Heat oil in skillet and fry until lightly golden on both sides. Remove fish from skillet. Pour marinade into skillet; bring to boil and serve with fish.

SPANISH CODFISH

1-1/2 to 2 cups shredded codfish
2 small round onions, sliced
1 medium green pepper, sliced
1 clove garlic, grated
4 large potatoes, sliced
1/4 cup tomato sauce

Fry green pepper, onion and garlic until golden. Add codfish and potatoes and cook until almost done. Add tomato sauce and continue cooking until potatoes are done. Serve with chips or crackers.

NOTE: The salt from the codfish gives it enough seasoning. Good as main dish also.

STUFFED CHIKUWA

2 chikuwa
1/4 lb. ground pork
1 slice ginger, minced
2-3 stalks minced green onion
3-4 water chestnuts, minced
1 large dried mushroom, soaked to soften and minced
1/2 tsp. cornstarch
1 tsp. shoyu
1 tsp. mirin

Peel loose skin from chikuwa, cut into fourths and cut each piece into half lengthwise. Make stuffing with remaining ingredients and stuff the chikuwa pieces.

Batter:
1/2 cup flour
1 egg, beaten with enough water to make 1/2 cup of liquid

Dip each piece of stuffed chikuwa into batter and deep fry until golden brown.

Sauce:
1 cup soup stock
2 Tbsp. shoyu
2 Tbsp. vinegar
2 Tbsp. cornstarch
2-1/2 Tbsp. sugar
1/2 tsp. hot Korean sauce

Bring the above to a boil and pour over deep-fried chikuwa or use as dipping sauce.

NOTE: When measuring 1/2 tablespoon, dip your tablespoon into the sugar straight up and down until you hit the center of the tablespoon. Gently lift out and you will note that the sugar will remain in the spoon. Sure beats having to measure 1-1/2 teaspoons.

SWEET-SOUR FISH CHUNKS

1 lb. mahimahi or swordfish
1/2 cup shoyu
1 Tbsp. rice wine
3 Tbsp. sugar
1 tsp. grated ginger
1 clove garlic, grated
2 eggs, beaten with water
Bread crumbs

Cut fish into 1-inch x 1-inch cubes and marinate in remaining ingredients 4 hours or overnight. Dip chunks in bread crumbs, then the beaten egg mixture and then in bread crumbs again and deep fry. Place fish chunks in serving bowl and pour sweet-sour sauce over them.

SWEET-SOUR SAUCE

1/2 cup brown sugar
1/2 cup pineapple juice
1/4 cup Japanese vinegar
2 Tbsp. cornstarch

Bring sugar, vinegar and pineapple juice to a boil. Add cornstarch that has been mixed with a little water and bring to a boil to thicken. Pour over deep-fried fish chunks and serve with toothpicks.

NOTE: Do not stir or mix once you have poured the sauce over it. You do not want the chunks to break apart.

BAKED MULLET

3 large mullets cut into 2- to 3-inch pieces
2 sticks butter, melted
2 tsp. lemon juice
2 tsp. mirin
4 Tbsp. shoyu
Sesame seeds
Chopped green onion

Sprinkle fish lightly with rock salt in a roasting pan. Mix remaining ingredients to make sauce. Pour over fish and and bake at 350° for 30 minutes, turning and basting a few times.

SMOKED ULUA

1 ulua, 6-8 lbs.
1 Tbsp. rice wine
2 tsp. salt
4 Tbsp. soy sauce
1 Tbsp. sugar
4 stalks green onion, smashed
4 slices ginger root
1/2 cup tea leaves
2 Tbsp. sugar
1/2 cup mayonnaise

Clean fish and cut into 4 sections; mix with wine, salt, soy sauce, sugar, green onion and ginger root. Let it marinate for one hour. Lightly oil grill or roasting rack; place fish on it. Preheat oven to 450°; place fish on grill in oven. Directly beneath grill place the tea leaves and sugar that have been placed in a pie pan or ovenproof plate and bake for 25 minutes. Remove fish to serving plate; brush outside lightly with sesame oil. Portion mayonnaise onto serving plate and serve.

NOTE: Aroma from tea and sugar will give fish a delicious smoky flavor. Any type of fish can be used.

SWEET-SOUR FISH CUBES

1/2 lb. fish fillets cut into 1-in. cubes
1 tsp. oyster sauce
1 tsp. cornstarch
1 tsp. salad oil
1 tsp. shoyu
1/2 tsp. sugar
1/2 tsp. sesame oil

Combine above and marinate for half an hour.

1 egg, slightly beaten
1 tsp. water
1/2 tsp. salad oil
1/2 cup cornstarch

Combine and add to fish mixture.

Heat oil for deep frying. Drop fish cubes in hot oil and cook about 30 seconds. Remove and drain on paper towel.

Sauce:
1/3 cup cider vinegar
1/2 cup catsup
1 6-oz. can pineapple juice
1/2 cup sugar
1 tsp. minced ginger
1 Tbsp. Sherry
1 Tbsp. cornstarch

Bring above to boil and pour over deep-fried fish cubes.

PAN-FRIED FISH PARMESANA

1 Tbsp. lemon juice
1 Tbsp. Worcestershire sauce
2 pounds fish fillets cut into bite-sized pieces
Salt and pepper to taste
1/2 cup flour
3 eggs, lightly beaten
1 cup grated Parmesan cheese
3 Tbsp. butter
2 Tbsp. vegetable oil

Combine lemon juice and Worcestershire sauce. Sprinkle on fish pieces. Salt and pepper the fish, then dredge lightly in flour. Dip fish in eggs, then coat generously with grated cheese. In heavy skillet sauté the fish in butter and oil mixture over medium heat for 3-4 minutes to brown. Turn and brown other side.

NOTE: I use lobster in place of the fish for a change sometimes when I want to splurge. You can cut the lobster into smaller pieces without worrying about it breaking up.

FISH BALLS IN TOMATO SAUCE

1 lb. fish fillets
1 tsp. salt
1/4 tsp. black pepper
1/4 tsp. sesame oil
1/2 Tbsp. cornstarch
1 medium round onion
3 cups oil
6 1-in. sections green onion
6 slices ginger root
3 Tbsp. tomato catsup
1/2 Tbsp. sugar
1 tsp. sesame oil
1 tsp. cornstarch
2 Tbsp. water

Score fillets lengthwise and crosswise; cut into bite-sized pieces and mix with salt, black pepper, sesame oil and cornstarch and let stand for 20 minutes. Cut onion into bite-sized pieces. Heat oil for deep frying; deep-fry fish pieces and onion pieces over medium heat for one minute; remove and drain. Remove all but 1 Tbsp. oil from pan; reheat oil and stir-fry green onion and ginger until fragrant; add catsup, sugar, sesame oil, cornstarch and water. When liquid comes to a boil, add fish meat and onion; mix together and add 1 tsp. fried oil. Toss lightly to mix all ingredients and coat fish slices with sauce; remove to serving plate.

NOTE: This is actually a main-dish recipe, but it makes an interesting pupu also.

TUNA-PUFF WEDGES

1 7-oz. can tuna, drained and flaked
1-1/2 tsp. prepared mustard
1/4 tsp. Worcestershire sauce
1/4 cup mayonnaise
1-1/2 tsp. grated onion
2 Tbsp. green pepper, chopped
3 hamburger buns or English muffins, split
1/2 cup mayonnaise
1/4 cup American cheese, shredded
6 tomato slices

Blend first 6 ingredients; pile onto bun halves. Top each half with a tomato slice. Blend 1/2 cup mayonnaise with the cheese and spread over tomato slices. Broil until topping puffs and browns.

When slightly cooled, cut into 4-6 wedges with a sharp knife and serve.

NOTE: You will not believe how delicious the lowly tuna can taste. Grated onion with mayonnaise does wonders for this recipe and other dips. Add enough onion so you can taste it. I found the Japanese plastic grater best for grating.

Always taste as you follow any recipe, making changes according to your taste. Mark the changes on your recipe immediately before you forget.

DEEP-FRIED FISH CAKE ROLLS

1 cup fish cake base	1/2 tsp. salt
1/4 cup water chestnuts, minced	1/2 tsp. cornstarch
1/2 cup minced ham or pork	1/2 tsp. shoyu
1 Tbsp. green onion, minced	1/2 tsp. liquor

Combine all ingredients and mix well. Divide into two parts and shape into a roll about 1-1/2 inches in diameter. Place on greased pan and steam 15 minutes.

Batter:

1 egg	1/4 tsp. salt
3 Tbsp. flour	Bread crumbs or cracker meal
1 Tbsp. water	Oil for frying

Dip rolls into batter made with egg, flour, water and salt. Roll in bread crumbs or cracker meal and deep fry until lightly golden. Drain oil. Slice and serve.

NOTE: For variation, wrap in nori before dipping into batter and fry. Rolls can be frozen after steaming. Thaw, dip in batter and fry when ready to use.

FRIED FISH CAKES

2 beaten eggs	1/3 cup grated Parmesan
2 cups surimi (fish cake base)	cheese
4 slices bacon, crisped and crumbled	1/4 tsp. salt
1/4 cup finely chopped green onion	1/8 tsp. pepper
2 Tbsp. finely chopped round onion	2 Tbsp. cooking oil

In bowl combine eggs, surimi, crumbled bacon, green onion, round onion, cheese, salt and pepper. Cover and chill at least 1 hour. Using 1/4 cup mixture for each, shape into patties about 3 inches in diameter. In large skillet cook patties in hot cooking oil over medium heat for about 5 minutes per side or until patties are set and golden.

NOTE: The cheese in this recipe gives it a very nice and distinctly different flavor.

MEATS

BARBECUED BRISKET ON BUNS

3 lbs. brisket of beef
1 cup catsup
1 tsp. salt
2 cups water
1/3 cup Worcestershire sauce

1/2 tsp. Tabasco
1 tsp. chili powder
1 tsp. liquid smoke
1 small onion, chopped
1/2 cup brown sugar

Cook brisket, uncovered, in a 350° oven for 2 hours. Mix remaining ingredients; pour over the meat and cook, covered, another 2 hours at 300°.

Cover and refrigerate meat and sauce overnight in the refrigerator.

The next day, slice the meat paper-thin; place the slices in a flat pan overlapping; cover with the sauce and heat in a 300° oven. Serve with dinner rolls or buns.

NOTE: When a recipe calls for a baking pan to be covered in the oven, use heavy-duty foil and crimp the edges securely. This will keep the heat within the pan, and the end result is a softer, juicer roast. This brisket is also good enough to be used as a luncheon dish.

BARBECUED BEEF STRIPS

2 lbs. flank steak
1 medium yellow onion, peeled
    and thinly sliced
2 bay leaves, crushed
10 whole black peppercorns
1 cup Marsala (wine)
2 cloves garlic, minced

1/4 tsp. white pepper
3 Tbsp. brown sugar
1/4 cup shoyu
1/3 cup olive oil
1 small bunch cilantro (Chinese
    parsley)
3-4 sprigs thyme

Cut steak crosswise at a 45° angle to make strips 1 x 1/8 x 5-6 inches wide. Set aside.

Combine remaining ingredients in large mixing bowl, add meat strips and marinate overnight in the refrigerator.

Weave 5-inch skewer into each strip and grill 4-5 minutes, turning once.

GRILLED SIRLOIN WITH SESAME

1 Tbsp. sesame seeds
1 Tbsp. sesame oil
1 tsp. ginger, minced
1 clove garlic, minced
1 scallion, both white and green parts, minced
1-2 Tbsp. honey
3/4 cup shoyu
Freshly ground pepper
2 lbs. boneless sirloin, cut in 2-inch strips

Toast sesame seeds over low heat in frying pan, stirring constantly until golden. Remove from frying pan and combine with sesame oil, ginger, garlic, scallions, honey to taste, shoyu and pepper to taste.

Add sirloin to shoyu mixture and marinate for at least 2 hours in the refrigerator. While marinating sirloin pieces, soak bamboo skewers in cold water to prevent them from burning.

Skewer one or two pieces, spaced slightly apart, and grill until partially done. Do not overcook pieces or they will become dry.

Garnish plate with parsley, place grilled sirloin skewers on it, and serve.

STIR-FRIED BEEF WITH LETTUCE

4 medium shiitake (Japanese black) mushrooms
1-1/4-lbs. ground beef
4 oz. bamboo shoots, coarsely minced
2 cloves garlic, finely minced
2 slices ginger, finely minced
4 water chestnuts, coarsely minced
1 stalk scallion (green onion) chopped
4 Tbsp. peanut oil
1 tsp. salt
1/4 tsp. pepper
1 Tbsp. light shoyu
1/2 Tbsp. black bean paste
1/2 Tbsp. hoisin sauce
1/2 Tbsp. sugar
1 Tbsp. rice wine or dry Sherry
1-1/2 tsp. sesame oil
2 sprigs parsley to garnish
12 lettuce leaves

Remove and discard stems from mushrooms soaked in hot water for 30 minutes. Coarsely mince the caps. Fry beef until browned; drain fat. In hot oil stir-fry ginger and mushrooms for 30 seconds before adding bamboo shoots, garlic and water chestnuts. After 1 minute add scallions and meat together with the salt and pepper. Cook another 2 minutes, stirring constantly. Add the shoyu, bean paste, hoisin sauce, sugar and rice wine and cook another 3 minutes. Add sesame oil and serve garnished with sprigs of parsley. People will help themselves to a couple of spoonfuls of the minced mixture by placing it on a lettuce leaf, wrapping it up carefully and eating it with their fingers.

BEEF SASHIMI

2 lbs. fillet of beef

Marinade:
2 round onions, thinly sliced
2 cloves garlic, thinly sliced
4 thin slices lemon
1/2 cup plus 2 Tbsp. rice vinegar
1/2 cup shoyu
1/4 cup rice wine (sake)

Barbecue the fillet on charcoal or broil in the oven approximately 4 minutes on one side and 3 minutes on the other DO NOT OVER-COOK. Plunge beef in ice water to stop cooking process and wash off any burned parts. Pat dry and set aside.

Combine all marinade ingredients in a large plastic bag. Place the fillet in the bag and seal, removing all air from the bag. This will eliminate having to turn the meat periodically. Refrigerate for 24 to 36 hours.

Remove the fillet from the marinade, slice thin against the grain and serve at room temperature. The inside should be medium rare.

NOTE: This is a very tasty and completely different way to serve beef. Use lean tenderloin and broil off the fat to reduce worries about cholesterol. Just remember that the fillet must be marinated 2 to 3 days, so do plan ahead. You will be well rewarded for your efforts.

DRIED BEEF CHUNKS

1-1/2 lbs. boneless beef shoulder
2 Tbsp. corn oil
2 Tbsp. sugar
1/4 to 1 cup water
1 tsp. shallots, chopped*

1 Tbsp. Galliano
1/4 to 1/2 tsp. cayenne pepper
1/2 tsp. salt
2 Tbsp. shoyu
Garlic salt

Preheat oven to 200°. Cut beef into 3/4-inch cubes, trimming off all fat. Heat oil in frying pan and add sugar and beef cubes. Sear and sugar-coat the beef for 4-5 minutes. Stir in remaining ingredients except garlic salt. Bring to a boil and reduce heat to medium. Cover and cook 30 minutes, stirring frequently. During the last 5 minutes, remove the cover and let most of the liquid evaporate. Transfer beef to a baking sheet and lightly sprinkle with garlic salt. Reduce oven temperature to 175° and dry beef for approximately 45 minutes. Turn off heat and let beef cubes cool in the oven. Store in a covered container in the refrigerator. Will keep for days in the refrigerator.

*Shallots look like miniature, elongated round onions and have a strong onion flavor. Use round onion if unable to find shallots.

NOTE: This freezes very well. Thaw to room temperature and serve with colored cocktail picks. Garnish with parsley sprigs.

SWEDISH MEATBALLS

1/2 cup fine, dry bread crumbs
1 cup light cream, warmed
1/2 lb. ground beef
1/2 lb. ground veal
1/2 lb. ground pork
2 egg yolks, slightly beaten

2 Tbsp. onion, finely chopped
1-1/2 tsp. salt
1/4 tsp. pepper
1/2 tsp. sugar
3 Tbsp. butter, melted

Soak crumbs in warmed cream for 5 minutes. Add meats and mix well. Add remaining ingredients; mix well and shape into 1-inch balls. Bake meatballs in single layer in preheated 350° oven until evenly browned. Serve with any sweet-and-sour dipping sauce.

MEATBALLS WITH GRAPE JELLY

1 lb. ground beef
1 egg
2 Tbsp. bread crumbs
Salt, pepper, onion salt and garlic salt to taste

Mix above ingredients and shape into balls smaller than walnuts. Set aside.

1 12-oz. bottle catsup
1 6-oz. jar grape jelly
Juice from 1 lemon

Mix above ingredients and melt in heavy skillet.

Place meatballs in rows in the skillet and cook covered for 30 minutes and uncovered for another 15 minutes.

Remove meatballs to a covered bowl and refrigerate. Freeze sauce so you can easily remove grease that floats to the surface. When ready to serve, heat sauce once again and add meatballs. Warm and serve.

NOTE: The sauce is just great. Cholesterol-watchers can use ground turkey and egg substitute.

BURRITOS

MEATS

1 lb. ground beef
1 bell pepper, chopped
1 whole green chili, seeded and chopped
1-2 stalks celery, chopped
1/4 tsp. pepper
1/4 tsp. salt
1/2 tsp. oregano
1/2 tsp. coriander
2 cloves garlic, chopped
15-oz. can Hormel chili, no beans
16-oz. can Rosarita refried beans
24 6-inch flour tortillas

Brown meat in saucepan. Add next 8 ingredients with 1/4 cup water and simmer 1-1/2 hours until tender. Add more water if necessary to prevent burning. Drain excess liquid when cooked.

Add chili and refried beans. Mix well. Place heaping tablespoonful on a tortilla, roll once, fold in both edges and continue rolling. Place seam side down in a baking dish and bake for 40 minutes in a 250° oven.

NOTE: There was some filling left over, so I wrapped it in won ton pi and fried it. It was simply delicious! Be certain to seal the pi completely so filling will not spill out and splatter in the hot oil. Cook over medium heat so it will be nicely browned and crisp. Enjoy! One cup of filling makes 20 burrito won tons.

TERIYAKI MEATBALLS

1-1/2 lbs. ground beef
2 eggs
2 Tbsp. flour
1 tsp. salt
Dash of pepper
2 Tbsp. cornstarch

1/4 cup sugar
1/3 cup shoyu
14 oz. beef broth
1/4 cup sake
2 Tbsp. minced ginger
2 tsp. minced garlic

Combine beef, flour, eggs, salt and pepper. Mix lightly and shape into small balls. Place in greased baking pan and bake at 400° for 14-17 minutes. Mix cornstarch, sugar, shoyu, beef broth, sake, ginger and garlic and cook until thick. Add meatballs and simmer.

Makes about 50 meatballs. Mix lean and 25-30%-fat ground beef equally for better flavor.

NOTE: The meatballs can be made ahead and frozen. Thaw and heat in the sauce and serve. Instant pupu.

TERIYAKI MEAT ROLLS

1 egg
1 lb. lean ground meat
1 pkg. teriyaki sauce powder
1/4 cup grated carrots

1 small round onion, chopped
4 sheets sushi nori
Bread crumbs
Oil

Mix ground meat, egg, teriyaki sauce powder, carrots and onion. Divide into four equal parts. Spread each portion onto one sheet of nori as you would when rolling sushi, starting with a thin layer closest to you and ending about 1-1/2 inches from the top end of the nori. Refrigerate rolls until firm, about 2-3 hours, or freeze them if you are in a hurry. Cut each roll into 10-12 slices, coat cut ends with bread crumbs and fry until nicely browned.

NOTE: These can be made ahead and frozen, cut when partially thawed, and fried. They may also be fried and then frozen for ready pupus on hand.

CHINESE MEATBALLS

1 lb. ground beef
3/4 cup minced celery
3/4 cup finely chopped almonds
1 clove garlic, minced
1 tsp. salt
1/2 cup bread crumbs
1 Tbsp. soy sauce
2 eggs, beaten
Cornstarch
2 Tbsp. cooking oil
Pineapple sauce

Combine beef, celery, almonds, garlic and salt; mix well. Add crumbs, soy sauce, and eggs and mix well. Shape into balls the size of walnuts. Roll in cornstarch. Heat oil in large skillet and brown meatballs on all sides until thoroughly cooked. Serve with Pineapple Sauce.

PINEAPPLE SAUCE

1/3 cup sugar
3 Tbsp. cornstarch
1 cup chicken broth
1/2 cup vinegar
2 Tbsp. soy sauce
1/2 cup pineapple juice
1 green pepper, cut into strips (optional)
1 cup pineapple chunks

In saucepan combine sugar and cornstarch. Stir in broth, vinegar and soy sauce to make smooth paste. Stir in pineapple juice; cook over medium heat, stirring constantly until thickened and clear. Add green pepper and pineapple chunks; simmer for 2 minutes. Pour over meatballs and serve immediately.

NOTE: The chopped almonds give it a very nice flavor and crunch, and served with the sweet-sour pineapple sauce, it is delicious. Your guests will love it.

HAMBURGER CROQUETTES

2 large potatoes, boiled
2 Tbsp. butter
1 lb. ground meat
1 tsp. salt
3 Tbsp. sugar
3 Tbsp. shoyu
Dash of pepper

Mash the potatoes while hot and add butter, mixing well to blend. Add remaining ingredients, mix well and form into croquettes. Dip croquettes in flour, egg, and then bread crumbs and deep fry until golden brown.

Makes 30-35 croquettes.

NOTE: To form croquette, roll a heaping tablespoon of the mixture in the palms of your hands to form a ball. Roll around about six times and then gradually add pressure to elongate it. There you have a croquette. This mixture can also be made into balls, which may be more pupuish than croquettes. This is also a very nice potluck dish that won't get greasy or need warming up.

BEEF SALAMI

4 lbs. ground beef
2 cups water
4 tsp. liquid smoke
1 tsp. onion powder
1/2 tsp. garlic powder
2 tsp. mustard seed
2 tsp. peppercorns (optional)
5 Tbsp. meat curing salt

Mix all above ingredients and shape into three rolls. Wrap in foil, shiny side in. Refrigerate 24 hours. Poke holes in foil, place in broiler pan and bake at 325° for 1-1/2 hours. Refrigerate, slice and serve.

KOREAN FLANK STEAK

1 flank steak (tenderized by butcher)
1/2 cup sugar
1/2 cup soy sauce
2 stalks green onion, chopped
1 clove garlic, minced
2 Tbsp. sesame seed, ground
1 Tbsp. sesame oil
2 eggs
Flour

Cut flank steak into 2-inch slices and marinate in remaining ingredients, except eggs and flour. Soak for at least 30 minutes. Coat each piece with flour, dip in egg and fry in just enough hot oil so meat won't burn. Add more oil as needed. Serve plain or with dipping sauce made with shoyu, sugar and vinegar to taste with a little chopped green onion.

NOTE: The whole steak can be marinated and fried. Very good potluck dish.

TOASTED CORNED BEEF SQUARES

1 cup mayonnaise
1 tsp. sugar
1/4 cup grated Parmesan cheese
1 tsp. seasoned salt
1/8 tsp. garlic powder
1/2 can corned beef
6 slices bread, cut into fourths and toasted

Mix first five ingredients and refrigerate for 24 hours. Mix with 1/2 can corned beef and spread on untoasted side of bread squares that have been previously toasted. Broil 3-4 minutes until bubbly.

NOTE: Can be made ahead and frozen either before or after broiling.

NEGI MAKI
(Beef and Scallion Rolls)

8-10 green onions, trimmed to 2- to 3-inch lengths
1/2 lb. top sirloin, sliced paper thin and cut into 8-10 5- x 2-in.
   pieces, trimmed of fat
1 Tbsp. vegetable oil
2 Tbsp. soy sauce
1 Tbsp. sugar
1 Tbsp. sake
1 Tbsp. dashi or stock
1 Tbsp. mirin

Divide green onion pieces evenly into 8-10 groupings. Roll slice of beef
around 1 group of onions. Secure with toothpick or tie with string.
Repeat. Heat oil in heavy large skillet over medium-high heat. Add
beef rolls, seam side down, and sauté 1 minute. Continue sautéing,
shaking pan to brown evenly. Reduce heat and add soy sauce, sugar,
sake and stock. Cook 2 minutes. Remove meat using slotted spoon. Let
cool slightly. Meanwhile cook pan juices over medium-high heat until
reduced by half. Discard toothpicks or string from rolls. Return rolls to
skillet. Add mirin and shake pan constantly until meat is well glazed.
To serve, cut each roll into 1/2-inch rounds and thread on skewer.
Arrange on serving platter.

NOTE: This looks very nice and is a unique way of serving onions.

RULLEPOLZE

9- x 7-in. flank steak
1/2 lb. veal, cut into 1-in. cubes
1/2 lb. pork, cut into 1-in. cubes
Salt and pepper
2 tsp. ground ginger or 1 tsp. ginger powder
1 cup grated round onion
1/4 cup sugar

Two or three days ahead, spread steak on board and pound thin. Cover with veal and pork cubes and sprinkle generously with salt and pepper. Add ginger and onions. Fold steak over and sew edges to keep filling inside. In dutch oven or large saucepan combine 1 cup rock salt, 1/4 cup sugar and 2 quarts water. Bring to boil. Add meat and boil for 5 minutes. Cool liquid with steak in it. Remove steak, place in large container (nonmetallic) and cover with cooled solution. Marinate 2-3 days. When ready to use, remove steak from marinade. In dutch oven or heavy saucepan bring 2 quarts of water and 2 tsp. rock salt to boil. Add steak; cover and simmer over low heat for 2 hours or until tender. Remove steak from liquid; place meat in large plate and top with cutting board on which heavy weight has been placed to flatten the meat. Chill for 2-3 hours. To serve, cut into very thin slices.

NOTE: This is of Scandinavian origin. It sounds very complicated, but really isn't. You will like the results.

CHINESE POTSTICKERS

Meat Filling:
1-1/2 lbs. ground pork
6 Tbsp. soy sauce
6 green onions, minced
2 Tbsp. dried shrimp, soaked and minced
3 Tbsp. shrimp water
1 Tbsp. sesame oil
1 Tbsp. peanut oil
1/4 tsp. grated fresh ginger
1 egg
2 cloves garlic, minced
1-1/2 lbs. Chinese cabbage
2 tsp. salt
60 won ton pi

Mix together well pork, soy sauce, green onion, dried shrimp, shrimp water, sesame oil, peanut oil, ginger, egg and garlic. Set aside. Core cabbage and chop fine. Cover cabbage with salt, mix lightly and let sit for one hour. Press out as much of the water as possible and add cabbage to meat mixture. Mix well.

Place about 2 teaspoons of meat in the corner of a won ton pi that has been cut into a circle by rounding off the corners. Fold in half, moisten the edges with beaten egg yolk and bring edges together, pressing gently to seal.

Heat two large heavy skillets with 4 tablespoons of oil in each. Place potstickers upright, close together in each skillet, seam side up. Sauté over medium heat for 2-3 minutes, cover to steam so won ton pi will become opaque, add 1/4 cup water in each skillet and continue cooking until most of the liquid disappears. Potstickers will burn slightly on the bottom. Remove gently with spatula and separate as you place them on the serving platter. May be served plain or with a dipping sauce made with a combination of vinegar, hot oil and shoyu to taste.

NOTE: If you like hot, peppery things, you may add a dash of Tabasco to the dip. As the name implies, they stick to the pot and leave a mess to clean up, but they are very good. Soak the pan in water and cleanup will be a breeze.

GYOZA

1 lb. ground pork
4 cloves garlic, minced
2 Tbsp. minced green onion
2 Tbsp. minced chives
1/8 tsp. sesame oil

1/8 tsp. salt
1 Tbsp. shoyu
1 egg
40 won ton pi

Mix everything together well. Place 1 heaping teaspoon on won ton pi and seal. Place in frying pan with about 2 tablespoons oil, cover and cook until bottom is crisp. Top will be soft. Serve with dipping sauce.

DIPPING SAUCE

Combine 1/2 cup shoyu, 2 tablespoons mirin, 2 tablespoons rice vinegar, 2-4 drops of Tabasco sauce or chili pepper water and 1/4 teaspoon sesame oil.

SIU MAI

24 won ton pi wrappers
1/2 lb. ground pork
1/2 cup minced ham
1/2 cup surimi (fish cake base)
1 egg, slightly beaten
1/2 tsp. sugar
1/2 tsp. salt

Combine ingredients and place a heaping teaspoonful in middle of won ton pi wrapper. Bring up all ends like a flower and squeeze gently between thumb and fingers at the top of the meat mixture. Steam for 20 minutes.

NOTE: Place a wet cloth under and over the siu mai to prevent it from drying out as it steams. Freezes well and can be resteamed when needed or warmed in the microwave.

PEARL BALLS

6 oz. pork hash
1/2 Tbsp. rice wine
1 Tbsp. soy sauce
1/4 tsp. black pepper
1/2 Tbsp. cornstarch
2 Tbsp. chopped water chestnuts
1 Tbsp. chopped dried shrimp
1 tsp. chopped green onion
1 tsp. chopped ginger root
1 Tbsp. cornstarch
3/4 cup mochi rice
1/2 carrot
Chinese parsley for garnish

Mix pork hash with wine, soy sauce, black pepper and cornstarch. Stir vigorously for 3 minutes to combine ingredients thoroughly. Add chestnuts, dried shrimp, green onion, ginger and cornstarch. Rinse rice until water runs clear; place in water to cover and soak for one hour; remove and drain. Pour rice onto a flat plate and spread rice. Divide pork hash into 20 equal portions and roll each into 1-inch balls; roll balls in soaked rice to completely coat the outside of the pork hash ball. Place 1/2 inch apart on heatproof plate and steam over high heat for 30 minutes; remove. Shred carrots and sprinkle a pinch over each rice ball. Add a tiny parsley leaf for garnish and serve.

NOTE: After steaming there will be some liquid on the plate. Drain and garnish before serving.

WINE MEATBALLS

Serves 50

1 lb. lean pork
1 clove garlic
2 small onions
Sprig of parsley
3/4 tsp. nutmeg
1/4 tsp. cinnamon
1/4 tsp. allspice
1 tsp. salt
1/4 tsp. black pepper
3/4 cup Sherry
3/4 cup water
Cinnamon stick
2 cloves
1/2 cup brown sugar

Put pork, garlic, onions and sprig of parsley through meat grinder. Mix ground meat, nutmeg, 1/4 teaspoon cinnamon, allspice, salt, pepper and 1 tablespoon of the Sherry. Let stand for 2 hours. In palms of hands coated lightly with cooking oil, roll 1 level teaspoon of mixture into ball the size of a marble. Continue until all meat is formed into balls.

Put water, cinnamon stick, cloves and sugar in heavy frying pan. Bring to boil. Drop meatballs into boiling mixture. Add remaining Sherry. Cook over low heat until meatballs have turned dark brown and most of liquid has evaporated. Remove meatballs. Attach a bit of parsley to each one with cocktail pick.

NOTE: Instead of grinding meat, buy ground pork and mince garlic and onions.

CHINESE PORCUPINE BALLS

3/4 cup mochi rice
1 cup cold water
1 lb. ground pork
1 egg, slightly beaten
1 Tbsp. soy sauce
1-1/2 tsp. salt
1/2 tsp. sugar
4 dried mushrooms, soaked, chopped
1 tsp. ginger root, finely chopped
6 water chestnuts, finely chopped
1 green onion, finely chopped

Soak rice in water for 2 hours, drain thoroughly in sieve and spread on cloth towel to dry. Combine pork, egg, soy sauce, salt and sugar in mixing bowl; blend thoroughly. Add chopped mushrooms, ginger, water chestnuts and green onions. Form pork mixture into balls, using about 2 tablespoons per ball. Roll pork balls in rice, pressing down gently but firmly so rice sticks to meat. Arrange balls on platter and steam 30 minutes. Serve hot.

NOTE: Some water will accumulate in the platter. Drain immediately after steaming. Garnish each ball with a little grated carrot and one tiny leaf of parsley. It will look too nice to eat.

ORIENTAL MEATBALLS

1/4 lb. ground pork sausage
1/4 lb. cooked shrimp, finely chopped
1/4 cup water chestnuts, finely chopped
1/4 cup onions, finely chopped
2 Tbsp. shoyu
1/4 tsp. sugar
1 egg, slightly beaten

Combine all ingredients in a bowl. Shape into 1-inch balls and fry in preheated 350° oven until brown. Serve hot with Chinese hot mustard for dipping.

HOISIN SAUCE BABY RIBS

2 cloves garlic, minced
1 Tbsp. ginger, grated
2 tsp. horseradish sauce
1-1/4 tsp. cayenne pepper
3 Tbsp. brown sugar
1/4 cup molasses
1/2 cup hoisin sauce
1/2 cup dark soy sauce
1/2 cup red currant jelly
30 small pork ribs, trimmed of fat

Mix together all the marinade ingredients. Pour over the ribs in a plastic bag, remove all the air, seal and marinate in the refrigerator overnight.

Preheat oven to 375°. Put ribs on a rack over a foil-lined baking sheet. Bake, turning often and basting with the remaining marinade, until the ribs are a dark, golden brown, approximately 30-35 minutes. Serve hot or warm. Cut into one rib to see whether it is cooked.

NOTE: This is simply delicious and simple to do. Hoisin sauce and dark soy sauce are available in the Oriental section at most markets. Any red jelly will do if you cannot find currant (grape) jelly.

CHINESE ROAST PORK STRIPS

1 lb. pork tenderloin
3 Tbsp. shoyu
2 Tbsp. hoisin sauce
2 Tbsp. Sherry
1 Tbsp. brown sugar
1 clove garlic, crushed

Mix shoyu, hoisin sauce, Sherry, brown sugar and garlic. Marinate pork for 4 hours or overnight.

Place meat on a rack in a roasting pan. Pour 1/2 inch water into roasting pan. Bake at 300° for 1-1/2 hours.

Cut tenderloin into 1/2-inch strips and serve with toothpicks. Serve with Sweet-and-Sour Dipping Sauce.

SWEET-AND-SOUR DIPPING SAUCE

1 cup peach preserves
1/2 cup mango chutney
2 Tbsp. lemon juice
2 Tbsp. water

Place ingredients in a food processor and blend until smooth.

NOTE: This is a delicious sauce that is very versatile. Use it as a dipping sauce for all meats and poultry. You will love it.

GLAZED SAUSAGE BALLS

1/3 lb. pork sausage
3/4 lb. ground pork or beef
1/2 tsp. salt
1/2 tsp. dry mustard
1/2 tsp. coriander seeds (crushed)
1/4 tsp. ground allspice
1 egg, lightly beaten
1/4 cup fine dry bread crumbs
1/4 cup thinly sliced green onion
1/2 cup apple jelly
1/2 cup chutney, finely chopped
1 tsp. lemon juice

In a bowl stir together sausage, ground pork, salt, mustard, coriander, allspice, egg, bread crumbs and onion until well blended. Shape into 1-inch balls. (May be refrigerated or frozen at this point.)

Place meatballs (thaw if frozen) on rimmed baking sheet and bake uncovered at 500° for about 8 minutes or until well browned; drain.

In large frying pan over low heat, stir together apple jelly, chutney and lemon juice; cook, stirring, until jelly is melted. Add meatballs; then cover and simmer for another 8 to 10 minutes or until glazed. Transfer to a chafing dish to keep warm and serve warm.

NOTE: The rimmed baking sheet will keep oil from spilling over the edge and possibly causing an oven fire.

UPSIDE-DOWN PIZZA SQUARES

1/2 lb. raw Italian sausage	2 Tbsp. butter or margarine
1/2 cup green pepper, chopped	1 cup milk
1 small onion, chopped	1-1/2 cups flour
1 clove garlic, minced	3 eggs
1/2 tsp. dry basil	1 14-oz. jar Ragu quick pizza sauce
1/2 tsp. thyme leaves	1 cup Cheddar cheese, shredded

Remove sausage casing, crumble sausage and fry in skillet with next 5 ingredients. Add butter or margarine and when melted, pour mixture into 9- x 12-inch baking pan. In blender beat eggs with milk and gradually add flour. Pour this carefully over the sausage mixture. Carefully top with pizza sauce, then cheese. Bake at 425° for 15-20 minutes or until topping is puffy and bubbly.

Cut into bite-sized squares when slightly cooled and serve.

NOTE: The original "oven pancake" recipe called for 4 eggs. I eliminated one egg and added 1/2 cup flour when I tried this the second time. The recipe also called for the pizza sauce to be passed around or spread over the finished "pancake." I tried it as described above and hope you like the result.

PORK SAUSAGE CHEESE BALLS

1 lb. Hoffy pork sausage
1 cup Bisquick
6 oz. grated Cheddar cheese
1/4 cup chopped round onion

Combine above ingredients with hands. Form into quarter-sized balls and bake at 350° on a cookie sheet for 15-20 minutes until slightly golden.

NOTE: This freezes well. For variations, use ground round or ground chicken or turkey. When using turkey, you will need to add some seasoning to your taste.

SWEET-SOUR LINKS

1 lb. hot dogs
1/2 cup brown sugar
1 Tbsp. flour
1 tsp. dry mustard
1/2 cup pineapple juice
1/4 cup rice vinegar
1/3 cup white sugar
1 tsp. shoyu

Cut hot dogs into thirds or fourths and set aside. Place all other ingredients in a saucepan and bring to a boil. Put in hot dogs and boil for three minutes or until hot dogs become plump. Garnish with pieces of pineapple.

Simple and easy to do for quantity pupus.

HOT DOG BACON WRAP

1-1/2 lbs. hot dogs, cut in thirds
1 lb. bacon strips, cut in thirds
1/2 cup catsup
2 Tbsp. brown sugar
2 Tbsp. cider vinegar
1 Tbsp. soy sauce
1 Tbsp. Worcestershire sauce
1/2 tsp. prepared (hot dog) mustard

Wrap hot dogs with bacon and secure with toothpicks. Lay in single layer in baking pan. Mix remaining ingredients and pour over hot dogs. Bake for 30-35 minutes at 350°, turning once.

TOASTED BACON AND CREAM CHEESE ROLLS

8 oz. cream cheese
2 Tbsp. cream or milk
12 slices soft white bread
1 lb. bacon

Beat together cream cheese and cream in electric mixer.

Remove crusts from bread by stacking and cutting 4 slices at a time. Spread cream cheese mixture on each slice. Cut slices in half; then cut each half into 2 pieces. Also cut bacon into 2-1/2- to 3-inch strips.

Roll each piece of bread jelly-roll fashion with filling on the inside. Wrap a piece of bacon around each roll, making sure bacon completely covers the seam so cream cheese will not seep out. Secure with a toothpick.

Before serving, broil until bacon is crisp. Keep on warming tray and serve warm.

NOTE: These can be frozen very nicely after they have been rolled and secured. Thaw and broil as directed above. Do not use cellophane-tipped toothpicks or they will burn while broiling.

PIZZA SKINS

3 oz. cream cheese, softened
1/2 cup butter, softened
1-1/2 cups flour

2 cups instant mashed potatoes
4 strips bacon, crisped
1 cup Cheddar cheese, grated

Make crust by beating cheese and butter together. Add flour and blend well. Form dough into a ball, cover with plastic wrap to prevent it from drying out and refrigerate for at least 30 minutes.

Roll dough to fit the bottom and sides of an 8-inch round or 13- x 4-inch tart pan and bake at 450° for 7-10 minutes or until lightly browned at the edges.

When cool, fill with mashed potatoes, cover with Cheddar cheese and top with bacon bits. Bake at 350° for 5-7 minutes until cheese is melted. Cut into wedges or squares and serve warm or at room temperature.

NOTE: When crisping bacon, slice into thin slivers and fry until crisp. You will be surprised at how much more you get by doing it in this fashion. Much easier and less messy, too.

REUBEN ROLL-UPS

4 oz. Swiss cheese, grated
1 cup sauerkraut, very well drained

1/4 cup prepared mustard
30 slices pastrami

Combine Swiss cheese with the sauerkraut. Spread a thin layer of mustard on each pastrami slice. Heap a generous spoonful of the cheese-sauerkraut mixture on each slice of pastrami.

Roll the meat tightly and skewer it through the center with a cellophane-tipped toothpick.

Refrigerate until serving time.

NOTE: IF you prefer to heat this before serving, remove the cellophane-tipped toothpick, place seam side down on a baking dish and bake for 5 minutes at 350°. Serve immediately after reinserting pick to hold it together.

CRISP-COATED HAM BALLS

3 Tbsp. butter
2 cups ground cooked ham
1/2 tsp. Worcestershire sauce
1 medium onion, finely chopped
1 egg, lightly beaten
1 Tbsp. parsley, chopped
6 Tbsp. flour
1-lb. can sauerkraut
Salad oil

Batter:
1-1/3 cups flour
1/2 tsp. paprika
1 cup water

In large frying pan, melt the butter, add onions and sauté 5 minutes. Add flour and cook 3 minutes longer. Remove from heat and stir in ham, egg, well-drained and finely chopped sauerkraut, Worcestershire sauce and parsley. Blend well. Cool, cover and chill thoroughly. Combine flour, paprika and water for batter and beat until smooth. In deep pan, heat 1-1/2 to 2 inches oil. Shape chilled ham mixture into walnut-sized balls.

Dip each ball into batter, drain briefly and fry a few at a time in hot oil until golden, about 2 minutes. Remove with slotted spoon and let drain. Arrange cooked balls on a cookie sheet in a single layer and freeze. Then package airtight. To serve, heat frozen balls, uncovered, in a 400° oven for 15 minutes or until heated through. Makes 4-5 dozen appetizers.

NOTE: I love sauerkraut, and this is a very nice way of using it. You can't really tell that it is sauerkraut when it is done this way. This is another recipe that you can freeze and put away until you need it.

HAM ROLL-UPS

8 oz. cream cheese, softened
4 oz. diced green chiles
16 oz. sliced ham

Spread ham with cream cheese mixed with drained chopped chiles. Roll up jelly-roll fashion. Chill and cut into bite-sized pieces before serving with toothpick inserted in each piece.

NOTE: Can be made ahead and frozen up to two months.

TRIPLE-DECKER HAM AND CHEESE

3 oz. cream cheese, softened
6 ham slices (sandwich meat)
Dash of salt
1/4 tsp. Worcestershire sauce
1/8 tsp. paprika
1/2 tsp. Pickapeppa

Season softened cream cheese with salt, Worcestershire sauce, paprika and Pickapeppa. Spread on slices of ham and stack to make triple deck. Refrigerate and when ready to serve cut into 9 squares. Serve with cocktail picks.

NOTE: May also be rolled up jelly-roll fashion, refrigerated, cut into three or four pieces, skewered and served.

HEALTHY PUPUS

ANTIPASTO

1 cup catsup
1 cup chili sauce
1 cup water
1/2 cup olive oil
1/2 cup tarragon vinegar
1/2 cup lemon juice
2 cloves garlic, minced
2 Tbsp. brown sugar
1 Tbsp. Worcestershire sauce
1 tsp. horseradish
Dash of cayenne pepper
Salt to taste

1/2 head cauliflower, cut bite-sized
3 medium carrots, thinly sliced
2 stalks celery, diced
1/2 lb. small mushrooms, trimmed
1 8-oz. jar pepperoncini, diced
1 6-oz. jar artichoke hearts,
    quartered
3 7-1/2-oz. cans chunk tuna,
    drained
1 6-1/2-oz. can shrimp, drained
1-lb. can cut green beans, drained

Combine first 12 ingredients in saucepan and simmer for 3 minutes. Add cauliflower, carrots, celery, mushrooms, pepperoncini and artichoke hearts and simmer 20 minutes until tender but crunchy. Add tuna, shrimp and green beans. Simmer 5 more minutes.

Cool and refrigerate at least 24 hours. Serve with wheat crackers.

NOTE: Keeps in the refrigerator for at least 2 weeks. This recipe makes a large quantity, so if you are planning to serve a small group, cut the recipe in half. You may add or eliminate any nonseasoning ingredient according to your taste.

OATMEAL CRACKERS

3 cups old-fashioned oatmeal
1 cup mochiko
1/2 tsp. baking soda

1/2 tsp. salt
1 cup water
1/4 cup no-cholesterol margarine

Boil water and margarine. Add to dry ingredients and mix lightly. Roll dough into quarter-sized balls and roll on baking pan to less than 1/4-inch thickness. Bake at 375° for 15-20 minutes until lightly browned.

TUNA ANTIPASTO

1 6-1/2-oz. can water-packed
    tuna, drained
1 15-oz. can artichoke hearts,
    drained and quartered
3 green onions, sliced

1/4 lb. fresh mushrooms, sliced
1 8-oz. can tomato sauce
1 Tbsp. olive oil
1/4 cup red wine vinegar
1 clove garlic, crushed

Combine all ingredients; chill at least 6 hours before serving.

Serve with crusty French bread for dipping.

NOTE: For variation I have used artificial crab, boiled scallops and chunky kamaboko in place of tuna, which tends to get messy when you mix the ingredients.

TUNA-STUFFED CUCUMBERS

1 6-1/2-oz. can water-packed
    light tuna, drained and
    flaked
1/2 cup soft whole wheat
    bread crumbs (1 slice)
1 medium stalk celery,
    chopped fine
1/4 cup finely chopped sweet
    red pepper

1 green onion, chopped fine
8 oz. plain lowfat yogurt
1 Tbsp. minced parsley
2 tsp. lemon juice
2 Tbsp. reduced-calorie mayonnaise
1-1/2 tsp. peanut oil
1 tsp. Dijon or spicy brown mustard
1/8 tsp. black pepper
4 medium cucumbers

In small bowl mix all of the ingredients except the cucumbers and set aside. Halve each cucumber crosswise. Using a spoon, carefully scoop out the centers, leaving shells about 1/4-inch thick. Stuff the tuna mixture into each hollowed-out cucumber half.

Wrap in plastic and refrigerate at least 4 hours. Cut into 3/4-inch slices to serve.

NOTE: Stuffed cucumbers will get soggy if left over, so stuff only what you need to serve at one time.

The red pepper and green onion and parsley look very Christmas-y. Delicious, too.

STUFFED MUSHROOMS

1 lb. large fresh mushrooms
1/2 cup Oil and Vinegar Dressing
1 bunch fresh spinach
1/2 cup safflower mayonnaise
3 Tbsp. grated onion
1 Tbsp. lemon juice
6 oz. king crab leg meat
1/2 cup grated lowfat Cheddar cheese

Clean and stem mushrooms; marinate in Oil and Vinegar Dressing for 1 hour. Drain. Wash spinach leaves; shake, but do not dry. Cook covered in heavy skillet 2-3 minutes or until wilted. Drain; squeeze out excess moisture. Chop. Combine mayonnaise, onion and lemon juice. Toss with crab and spinach. Stuff mushrooms; sprinkle with cheese. Bake at 375° for 15 minutes.

NOTE: You may omit the spinach or omit the crab and double the spinach for those who are allergic to seafood.

OIL AND VINEGAR DRESSING:

1/2 cup safflower oil
1/4 cup olive oil
1/4 cup cider vinegar
3/4 tsp. or less salt
1/4 tsp. pepper

Combine ingredients in covered jar; shake. Yield: 1 cup.

MARINATED MUSHROOMS

1 lb. fresh mushrooms
Juice of 1 lemon
1 lemon, cut into thin rounds
3/4 cup safflower oil
1/4 cup cider vinegar
2 cloves garlic
1/4 tsp. pepper
1 tsp. or less salt
Fresh parsley for garnish

Clean mushrooms; trim stems. Place in a large saucepan; toss with lemon juice. Add oil, vinegar, garlic, pepper and salt. Cook over medium-high heat 20-30 minutes, stirring frequently.

Remove from heat; cool to room temperature. Chill. Drain. Cover a serving plate with fresh parsley; top with lemon rounds. Spoon mushrooms over lemons and serve.

NOTE: These mushrooms will keep about a week in the refrigerator. Remaining marinade can be used for marinating artichoke hearts or as a salad dressing.

MARINATED SALMON

1/2 cup fresh lime juice
3/4 cup onion, finely chopped
1 stalk celery, finely chopped
2 tomatoes, peeled and chopped
3/4 tsp. or less salt
3/4 tsp. pepper
1-1/2 tsp. sugar
3-4 drops Tabasco sauce
1 lb. fresh salmon, skinned, boned and cut into 1-inch cubes
Fresh parsley for garnish
Fresh lemon wedges for garnish
Cherry tomatoes, halved, for garnish
1 white onion, sliced into rings, for garnish

Combine lime juice, onion, celery, tomatoes, salt, pepper, sugar and Tabasco, and pour over salmon. Toss; cover.

Chill at least 6 hours; drain.

To serve, cover a bed of fresh parsley with onion rings. Arrange salmon over top; ring with cherry tomatoes and lemon wedges.

NOTE: Serve with French bread. For those who are cholesterol conscious, this is a good and healthy way to serve salmon.

DEVILED SHRIMP

12 black peppercorns
12 coriander seeds
4 whole cloves
1 bay leaf
1/2 tsp. each red pepper flakes, mustard seeds and crumbled dry
    thyme
1 medium yellow onion, chopped
1 small stalk celery, chopped
3 slices lemon
3 cloves garlic, sliced thin
2/3 cup white wine vinegar
24 large shrimp, shelled and deveined
1/4 cup lemon juice
1/4 cup shoyu
1/8 tsp. cayenne pepper to taste or hot red pepper sauce to taste

Place peppercorns, coriander seeds, cloves, bay leaf, red pepper flakes, mustard seeds and thyme in small piece of cheesecloth and tie securely. In a large heavy saucepan, bring 2-1/2 cups of unsalted water to a boil over moderately high heat; add the onion, celery, lemon slices, garlic, vinegar and bag of spices.

Reduce the heat to moderate and let mixture simmer uncovered for 15 minutes. Add the shrimp and cook, uncovered, stirring often for 2-3 minutes or until they turn pink. Transfer to a large bowl and cool to room temperature. Cover and refrigerate. Drain the shrimp and place in a serving dish. Add the lemon juice, shoyu, cayenne pepper and red pepper sauce and toss to mix. Serve with toothpicks.

HEALTHY PUPUS

TERIYAKI TOFU

1/4 cup sesame seed	1/4 cup firmly packed brown sugar
2 Tbsp. dry Sherry	1/4 tsp. dry mustard
2 tsp. cornstarch	1 tsp. grated ginger
1/3 cup shoyu	1 block fresh tofu
2 cloves garlic, pressed	

Cut tofu into thirds lengthwise. Drain and set aside. In small pan over medium heat, stir sesame seed until lightly toasted; remove from pan and set aside. In same pan, stir together Sherry and cornstarch; stir in shoyu, garlic, brown sugar, dry mustard and ginger and cook over medium heat until mixture boils and thickens; cool.

Fry tofu in hot oil until golden brown on both sides. Pour sauce over tofu in shallow pan and coat thoroughly on all sides; cover tightly with foil and marinate for 1 hour. Broil tofu on rack in shallow baking pan until sauce bubbles (about 2 minutes on each side), basting occasionally with remaining sauce. Cut into 3/4-inch cubes, sprinkle with sesame seed and serve with wooden picks for spearing.

NOTE: The original recipe called for aburage. I prefer tofu.

TOFU DIP/SANDWICH SPREAD

1/2 block tofu (approx. 10 oz.)	2 Tbsp. mayonnaise
1 Tbsp. green onion, minced	1/4 tsp. salt
2 tsp. garlic powder	White pepper to taste
1 Tbsp. French's mustard	

Squeeze excess water from tofu using cheesecloth or dishtowel. Mash well and mix with remaining ingredients. Use as a dip with vegetables or Oatmeal Crackers (page 158).

NOTE: When using as a sandwich spread, use 2 additional tablespoons of mayonnaise. Good with tomatoes and lettuce. Our daughter who hates tofu just loved this and sent the recipe from Honolulu.

MISCELLANEOUS

KONBU MAKI

4-5 feet kanpyo (dried gourd strips)
12 in. konbu (dried seaweed)
2 cups cold water
2 tsp. rice vinegar
1 cup dashi or water
2 Tbsp. sake
1-1/2 Tbsp. sugar
3 Tbsp. soy sauce
1 Tbsp. mirin

Combine kanpyo in bowl with enough warm water to cover and le'
soak 10 minutes. Squeeze kanpyo between hands. Rinse in cold wate'
and drain well. Return to bowl. Cover with cold water and let soak 5
10 minutes. Squeeze kanpyo again. Drain well; pat dry. Cut konbu intc
8-10 rectangles. Roll each tightly. Tie some kanpyo ribbon arounc
middle of each (use double knot) to resemble scroll. Cut all but 1 incl
off each end of kanpyo ribbon. Combine 1 cup cold water and 1 tsp
vinegar in large saucepan and bring to boil over medium-high heat
Add rolls, reduce heat and simmer 5 minutes, skimming any foam tha
accumulates on surface. Drain well. Repeat process with remainin;
cold water and vinegar. Drain well. Rinse saucepan and pat dry. Adc
dashi and sake and mix well. Add rolls, place over low heat and cool
5 minutes. Stir in soy sauce and cook 5 minutes. Blend in mirin
Increase heat to high and swirl liquid in pan to glaze rolls. Let cool t(
room temperature, swirling pan several times. Transfer rolls to servin;
platter.

NOTE: Very elegant-looking pupu. It is not as complicated as i
sounds.

MINIATURE KONBU RICEBALLS

2-1/2 cups hot cooked rice
2 1-1/4-oz. pkgs. shiofuke konbu

Cut konbu into small pieces. Mix well into hot rice and make miniature riceballs or elongated sushi rolls.

NOTE: Very good as musubi for picnics requiring very little okazu. It's salty, so take lots of soda.

TARO CAKE

2 cups taro, diced into 1/2-in. cubes
1 cup flour
3/4 cup water
1/2 cup chopped dried shrimp
1/2 cup diced char siu
1/4 cup finely diced ham
1/2 cup chopped green onion
2 Tbsp. Chinese parsley, chopped
1 tsp. salt
2 tsp. sesame seeds

Fry taro cubes in 2 tablespoons oil, cover, and simmer 5 minutes. Combine flour and water to form paste. Add all ingredients, including taro paste mixture, except sesame seeds. Grease 8-in. cake pan and spread mixture in pan. Place in steamer and steam for 25 minutes. Garnish with sesame seeds and shredded fried egg, if desired.

TOFU WITH EAST ASIAN SAUCE

2 blocks tofu
3 Tbsp. peanut butter
3 Tbsp. sesame oil
3 Tbsp. shoyu
1 Tbsp. rice vinegar
1 tsp. chili sauce
2 Tbsp. Sherry
1 tsp. sugar
1 tsp. hoisin sauce
2 tsp. plum sauce

Cut each block of tofu into 8 pieces. Place in heatproof dish and steam vigorously for 10 minutes. Heat all other ingredients in a small saucepan over gentle heat, stirring constantly for about 2 minutes. Pour the hot sauce evenly over the tofu.

NOTE: The sauce has a delightful flavor. I used chunky peanut butter and the pieces of peanut gave it a nice texture.

TOFU APPETIZER

1 block tofu
1/2 cup finely sliced sanbaizuke
1/2 cup finely shredded lettuce

Slice tofu in half horizontally and into 8 equal pieces. Place shredded lettuce and sanbaizuke on top of each piece and serve cold.

NOTE: Very refreshing. Can be used as a salad on a hot day when you don't want anything fussy. Use any type of pickle that you have at home.

TOFU SURIMI PUFFS

1 block tofu
2 cups surimi (fish cake base)
3/4 tsp. salt
Dash of ground ginger
2 sheets nori

Cut tofu into fourths. Place tofu, one piece at a time, in muslin dish-towel and squeeze as much of the water out as possible. Grind tofu in suribachi or in blender until fine. Add surimi (fish cake base) and seasoning. Cut nori into three strips lengthwise and each strip into 8-10 pieces. Scoop surimi-tofu mixture by spoonfuls and wrap a piece of nori around the center of each. Drop into deep hot oil and fry until delicately brown. Serve hot or cold.

NOTE: These will puff up while hot and shrink slightly when they have cooled. You may add vegetables and anything else you want and make this into a main dish or side dish. Chopped fresh shrimp give it a nice flavor also.

KOREAN ABURAGE

1 pkg. aburage
2-3 cloves garlic, mashed
3 Tbsp. Wesson oil or sesame oil
3 Tbsp. shoyu
2 Tbsp. rice vinegar

2 Tbsp. sugar
Sesame seeds, roasted and
   crushed
1 chili pepper, crushed

Cut aburage into slivers and marinate in remaining ingredients overnight. Add more shoyu if desired.

NOTE: The recipe doesn't call for it but I rinse the aburage in hot water three times before I sliver it. It takes out most of the oil in which it was cooked. When doubling the recipe, use 3 tablespoons of Wesson oil <u>and</u> sesame oil. Very easy and economical recipe. People will enjoy it.

CHINESE FRIED WALNUTS

6 cups water
4 cups walnuts
1/2 cup sugar
Salad oil
Salt

Heat water to boiling over high heat; add walnuts and heat to boiling. Cook for one minute. Rinse walnuts under running hot water; drain. Wash saucepan and dry well. In large bowl, with rubber spatula, gently stir warm walnuts with sugar until sugar dissolves. (If necessary, let mixture stand 5 minutes to dissolve sugar.) In saucepan over medium heat, heat 1 inch salad oil to 350° on deep-fat thermometer. With slotted spoon, add about half of walnuts to oil; fry 5 minutes or until golden, stirring often. With slotted spoon, place walnuts in coarse sieve over bowl to drain; sprinkle very lightly with salt; toss lightly to keep walnuts from sticking together. Transfer to paper towels to cool. Fry remaining walnuts. Store in tightly covered containers. Makes 4 cups.

MISCELLANEOUS